The Seq

KAREN WRIGHT

BIBLIOCAST
An Imprint of Word Keepers, Inc.

Library of Congress Control Number: 2005933172

ISBN 0-9649679-3-6

BIBLIOCAST
An Imprint of Word Keepers, Inc.

Publisher/Editor: Toni Dianne Holm
Cover and Interior Design: Heather Scott
Copy Editor: George E. Tice
Production Services: RPK Editorial Services, Inc.

Cover Image: Sun Breaking Through Redwood, ©Darrell Gulin/CORBIS

"The River" by Garth Brooks/Victoria Shaw
Copyright © 1991 BMG Songs, Inc. (ASCAP) /Major Bob Music, Inc. (ASCAP)/
Mid-Summer Music, Inc. (ASCAP). All rights reserved. Used by permission

Advanced Praise for The Sequoia Seed

"Strap yourself in for a deep, provocative, mind-altering, life-enhancing read from the mind and heart of a woman who lives her own life in alignment with the perennial truths she writes about."
–John Scherer, Author, *Work and the Human Spirit*, Washington

"When you're feeling lost and confused . . . when life stops making sense . . . when you know you can do, be and have more, and you need the practical answers that'll help you make it happen . . . that's when you need *The Sequoia Seed*."   –Pat Lynch, Author, *The Five Secrets*, Arizona

"This is FANTASTIC! You sure do have a way with words! I LOVE what you write, the truth and integrity it carries and the provocative, emotive prose you use! You are just MAGIC, Ms. Wright!"
–June Hope, Director, Training Consultancy, Australia

"Your writing is like a literary river that slowly, but persistently, wore away my doubts, blame and anger."
-Al Olsen, Financial Planner, Washington

"Your writing is refreshingly frank and you cut through the fluff with laser precision. It feels like I'm sitting across from a good friend at my kitchen table. I use your insight like a close friend's advice."
–Sonja Meline, Teacher, Minnesota

"Obstacles and frozen moments and frantic overwhelm. You have the antidote to all of those."   –Sandy Kay, Writer, California

"It amazes me that one person can be blessed with such wisdom. You always seem to grab me by the scruff of the coat and give me a little shake."   –Teresa Merryfield, Life Coach, Alberta, Canada

About the Author

Karen Wright's life is summed up in her favorite Marcel Proust quote, "The real voyage of discovery consists not in seeking new land-scapes, but in having new eyes." Her nomadic search for Self, seeking numerous careers and locales, became her soul's curriculum. Her many paths led to lessons in letting go of fear, listening to inner guidance, and coming home to her own spirit. It was an inner journey—a shift in per-spective—that prepared her to help others navigate that rocky course to spirit. "It is the longest journey and the shortest distance," she confides. "With a shift in thought, entire lives can change."

An acclaimed inspirational speaker and consultant to leaders, Karen opens new doors of possibility and partnership when confusion and stagnation threaten to demoralize teams and destroy personal lives. She teaches leaders how to earn employees' discretionary effort—the available, but rarely accessed, wealth of talent, creativity, and passion that all individuals possess.

Karen is the author of the internationally read "Waking Up," an inspi-rational and life changing, on-line e-zine with a fiercely loyal following. Her writing speaks of everyday challenges with self-worth, fear, and life purpose—encouraging us to embrace the unknown and recognize the greatness in us all.

Karen's study of chaos theory, quantum physics, and brain physi-ology led her to see that the fulfillment of our individual lives is inex-tricably connected to humanity's spiritual evolution. Her position is succinctly profound. "Whether we speak of countries or families, all life is one."

Karen resides in the Pacific Northwest—close to family and the nurturing sustenance of undisturbed natural beauty. You may contact her at: karen@wrightminded.com or visit her website at http://www.wrightminded.com.

Table of Contents

Finding your place in this life can test your spiritual foundation. But, in testing, you discover your true nature.

Life may appear complex and ever-changing, but truth is simple and constant. Learn how truth feels and stay on your path.

Overcome limiting habits and make easy, small steps that add up to huge wins every time.

Looking for answers? The quality of the question you ask determines the richness of the answer you're capable of hearing.

When the dream dies, regain your footing and soar even higher.

The greatest satisfaction in life is being who you really are in every moment. Why is it that that level of honesty scares us so?

Want to make a difference? Use these two simple words to transform you and the world.

Act Two: The Fires Come – sharpening your spiritual skills 45

Discover how fear, doubt, and confusion are actually some of your best friends.

Are you relying on discipline to make change happen? Discover the power of your subconscious and see lasting results.

Should you? Shouldn't you? Overcome indecision and learn a new way of making life-enriching decisions.

Chasing happiness? Find out how your approach may be defeating you.

Is your life stalled and going in circles? Find out how to release the brakes and achieve what you really want.

Are you good at manifesting lack? Rejoice! Learn how to create abundance with just a slight change in aim.

Foreword by Jim Warda

Karen Wright understands us, because she has looked deeply into herself, even the darkest places, and wasn't afraid to tell us what she found.

In *The Sequoia Seed*, like a kind and wise friend, Karen takes the time to sit with us, listens to our hopes and fears, and at the same time, gives us a good swift kick in the butt to remind us just how much we have to offer.

She believes in us and our ability to change.

She's an observer. She sees things in us we can't always see. She sees our strength. She sees our truth. She sees the things we want to hide, the sometimes shame, the sometimes regret, the oftentimes feeling that we won't be able to get it done. Yet she sees it all with caring eyes, letting us know there's nothing wrong with us. In fact, there's everything right with us.

She sees what we can be, and won't let us rest until we've become it.

The Sequoia Seed is a gift. It's Karen being the friend who calls on the phone at night, wanting to know how our day went, wanting to know what amazing things we accomplished, wanting to know what's been tough, wanting to help us stand up after a particularly hard fall. Then, when we tell her how rough it's been, she understands. When we laugh, she laughs. When we cry, she's just quiet and listens, which is exactly what we need exactly when we need it.

In these pages, you'll find her compassion. She understands we're all going through something, struggling to greatness, trying to be our best, wanting to love and be loved—forever and a day—and even a few minutes after that.

In these pages, you'll find her belief that we create our reality, and that we have the ability to punch holes through the walls of illusion we've also created to hide from the responsibility.

She knows there is dignity in the struggle, divinity in being human, divinity in losing our way and then finding it on a moonstruck night in June.

Her words are a poet's words—"To see truth, you must come from truth."

Her words are inspiring—"You are eternal. You are safe. You are stronger than anything this world visits upon you."

Her words are strong—"Ironically, what you heard was not, 'No.'

It was 'Know.'"

Her words are clear—"Life is not in the answer business. It, forever and always, asks questions."

Her words are thoughtful—"Behave yourself into becoming the person you wish to be."

Her words are her words. Yet, they're ours, too. Because, in many ways, Karen speaks for us.

As you read *The Sequoia Seed*, you'll find yourself constantly amazed by how Karen seems to know you, because she does. She knows what we're all going through. She knows it because she's going through it, too. Her gift is that she can take that knowing and put it into words. Glorious, grace-filled words.

Thank you, Karen, for the gift of this book. It came from your heart. I can tell.

–Jim Warda, Author, *Where Are We Going So Fast?*

Acknowledgements

They say it takes a village to raise a child—I've found it also takes a village to produce a book. More than I ever imagined, the creation of *The Sequoia Seed* mirrored the birth of a child. From conception to delivery, I have had a team of incredibly talented professionals—really midwives—guiding me through the evolution of the book you now hold. What was unexpected was the journey of personal growth as well. I am endlessly grateful.

To my loyal "Waking Up" subscribers, thank you for your years of dedication and striving to live fully and authentically. I have learned much from you, and I am delighted to call many of you my dear friends. Without you, this book would not exist.

To my Editor extraordinaire, Toni Dianne Holm, you are my hero. I'd hoped to find an editor that would understand my book. I am truly blessed to have found one that also understood me. You held my hand when I lost my way and reigned me in when I blindly charged at mirages. Without you, this book would not exist.

To my team of passionate author-makers—Heather Scott, Art Director, Rose Kernan, Production Editor, and George E. Tice, Copy Editor—thank you for your skill in polishing and primping *The Sequoia Seed* for its debut. Without you, this book would not exist.

To my loving family and dear friends who bore the weight of my alternating agony and elation throughout the creation of this book, thank you for your unwavering belief in my success. It made the journey more delicious. Without you, this book would not exist.

And finally, because it was most dear, I thank God for using my mouth and my life to make whatever difference I can in shining a light in the darkness we experience when our fires threaten to consume us. Without You, I would not exist.

Preface

It can grow taller than the Statue of Liberty and live nearly forty centuries. Ancient fossil remains show that its ancestors date back for 175 million years. The giant of its species is the most massive of all living forms on the planet. It would take twenty adults, holding hands with outstretched arms, to encircle its base. Yet, paradoxically, it begins as a tiny seed smaller than a flake of oatmeal. This is the mighty Sequoia tree.

Its egg-sized cone can lie undisturbed on the forest floor for fifty years before surrendering its seeds. Ironically, the forest fires that destroy other trees are friends to the Sequoia. Its four-foot thick bark chemically repels the flames, and the fire's heat opens the cone, to at last, release its seeds to take root.

Like the dormant Sequoia seed, our destinies are often set in motion by our own personal fires. A health crisis, the loss of a loved one, and the acceptance of a truth not before seen—these are the infernos that reduce our ideologies to ashes and give birth to new sight. These are the precious moments when we can release our grip on old realities and open ourselves up to the budding possibilities of a bountiful life.

This is the purpose of *The Sequoia Seed*: to cast seeds and embrace the fires—for they shall surely come, these struggles that transform our lives. The question is, will we bud or will we burn? Will we trust that life's abundance is our ever-present inheritance, or will we cling to the lie of unworthiness? Will we give this world our sacred gifts of contribution and passion, or will we die with our music still inside us?

Problems, difficult people, tragedies—these are our fires; these are our teachers. When the heat approaches we can choose to release or retreat. And that choice becomes our experience and fashions the fate of our lives. Each day we may choose again—to see with new eyes; to look beyond the illusion of limitation to the magnificence that we are!

This book's seeds lie in the inspirational and provocative insights of my on-line subscription-based e-zine, "Waking Up." For years, loyal readers throughout the world have received timely messages challenging them to give more, love deeper, and engage wholeheartedly with life. Hundreds wrote to tell me of their hurdles and their growth. Here, you'll read the stories of real people who've faced real dilemmas. People who have struggled with all the troubles you too may have faced. People who didn't have it all figured out, but kept walking anyway. Those who felt the pain and still got out of bed to take on another day because they learned to listen to their inner voice of wisdom over the barrage of world opinion. Life is not for the weak of spirit. It requires much. My respect and admiration for those who shared their stories with me is endless.

Unlike lighter reading, *The Sequoia Seed* is best enjoyed with time between readings since each chapter is intensely thought provoking. Some chapters will present new ideas to contemplate; others will pose questions that may trigger personal soul searching. It's best to let a chapter ripen for awhile—let it germinate and take root. View your reading as a journey through your mind and life to unearth old forgotten beliefs and discover new insights. Some chapters will ask you to dig in and immerse yourself in exercises. I encourage you to get involved and not skip through these opportunities so that you will have a richer experience. Isn't that what you're after?

The Sequoia Seed contains a series of three acts or parts that parallel our process of growth. Act One: The Cone Awaits, contains chapters that ask you to notice the self-identity you've created and how you are demonstrating that identity to the world. Act One is the beginning of growth toward wholeness. In Act Two: The Fires Come, you dig into how you navigate the journey of your life. Act Two will sharpen your spiritual skills and simplify your daily challenges. With the spiritual skills of Act Two in place, you'll now determine how to follow your heart and resolve your will. This is also a time of celebration and to remember what's most valued in this journey to wholeness. Act Three: The Mighty Sequoia Grows, our final section, glimpses destiny and explores the ripening of your purpose and path.

As you read, dare to question and to be accountable for the choices you've made and the life you've lived thus far. Owning your choices is the key to freedom. We can never really release anything until we fully take responsibility for it. This is where you'll begin to create with intention and return to the wholeness of your spirit.

On the path to spiritual evolution, what you do means far less than who you become. How did you manage your Self through the journey of life? Did you use your hardships to forge stronger determination and commitment? Did you learn that losses show up to prove that you never really lose anything that's truly yours?

Enjoy *The Sequoia Seed* time and time again. Each reading will prompt personal growth and in that growth you will find new insights in future readings. You'll see things that you will swear weren't there before because you'll be reading with new eyes. I'd love to hear about your experience of strolling through the forest of these pages.

Act One:
The Cone Awaits

-assessing your reality

1 # The Balancing Act

"We are not human beings on a spiritual journey.
We are spiritual beings on a human journey."
—Stephen R. Covey

Author's Note: Finding your place in this life can test your spiritual foundation. But, in testing, you discover your true nature.

High above, the tightrope walker gingerly places one foot on the rope, wiggles his foot to find the just-right position before shifting his weight from the platform onto the taut rope. With one foot still firmly planted on the landing, the first step out is the easiest.

Then, when the feel is right, he moves his second foot onto the rope, bobbling slightly as he finds his balance on the slender strand he will walk high above the crowd. Further and further away from the platform he inches; further and further from the steadiness of a securely anchored rope.

As the daredevil makes his way to the middle of the suspended rope, it begins to sway and bounce slightly. The rope is slack. The cable droops beneath his weight and each step of his progress is now uphill. His sole's grip must be firm or he will slide backward. He concentrates hard to keep a single focus of calm and balance. As he makes his way to the distant platform, the rope becomes increasingly steady and sure. Finally, he leaps onto the solid platform and the crowd releases a long-held collective sigh.

If we consider this experience through the lens of metaphor, we might glimpse a few very fundamental truths about our own journey through life--which you might agree can often feel like walking a tightrope.

Let's imagine that the platform represents our spiritual base. It is where we feel confident and secure. It is constant and unchanging, because truth is eternal. For this is a place of truth. Nothing is ambiguous or unstable. There is little risk. We feel self-assured and strong. There is no real reason to ever leave our spiritual home, but we humans often get restless. So, one day we step out onto the rope—toward a new experience.

No longer standing on the solid ground of what we *know*, we immediately feel a sense of apprehension—even fear. The ground is no longer still and every move we make triggers ripples of increasing turmoil. It is tough to keep our balance, and we often overreact to the swaying rope, causing it to swing even more wildly. If we were not afraid before, we are now.

Imagine that moving away from the steady platform is also moving away from our spiritual base. The further we stray, the more unstable we become. The confidence and strength of living in spirit fades with each step we take. Risks loom large and fear plagues our minds. It takes great focus and concentration to keep our balance and not fall. We can begin to doubt ourselves and forget that we are always safe— no matter what. We forget who we are.

Rachel's courageous experience below illustrates this metaphor with precision and humor. Having done a ropes course myself, I can attest to the authenticity of her fears!

"A friend of mine owns an adventure company that offers outdoor experiences to businesses and organizations looking for unusual team building exercises. I visited his camp one day and he invited me to join a group of high school students who were just beginning their ropes course. A ropes course is a series of outdoor challenges that tests your physical strength as well as your mental and emotional control. Each task is usually very simple, but profoundly difficult.

I had friends who had participated in ropes courses before and they always spoke of it as one of the most powerful and self-revealing experiences they'd ever had. So, when my friend invited me to join in, I agreed enthusiastically.

It didn't take me long to be reminded that these high school students were about thirty years younger than me. Funny how the mind forgets age, isn't it? While they seemed to do each challenge with ease, I struggled to hide my obvious lack in strength and mortal belief in danger.

In one particular experience my fear got the better of me. I don't remember what the task was called. I think panic wiped everything out except the fear. I remember THAT vividly! The goal was to climb a twenty foot vertical pole, stand on a platform at the top and leap six feet out to grab a hoop they called 'The Golden Ring.' What my friend didn't tell me was that the wooden steps hammered into the side of the pole were set in such a way that you couldn't easily climb up or that the platform at the top of the pole swiveled! Or the worst, that when you jumped for the ring, the pole I stood on would sway backwards defeating my push.

It's a good thing I didn't know these things before I began. Oh, I almost forgot—I was wearing a harness around my body that insured I would not fall to my death! This is a little fact that my mind would conveniently forget for the entire length of my ordeal.

The climb up the pole looked like a piece of cake. I wasn't the first one to do this challenge and I watched as kids one-third my age sprinted up like it was no big deal. But, it was a big deal! I got about half way up and found that the foot I was standing on was also the one I needed to reach the next available step. After much jockeying, I reached the platform.

Here was dilemma number two. The platform not only swiveled, but it was bigger around than the pole I clung to. Which meant that I had to let go of the pole and hoist myself over the lip of the platform to get to the top. And I finally did. None too gracefully, I'm afraid.

So, here I was, crouched on the platform with the students telling me to stand up. Remember, the platform swivels . . . and it also rocks. It's not a solid footing. Kind of like standing on a clipboard balanced on a little rock. Try as I might, I could not stand up. Squat was my position of choice. But, you can't jump from a squat!

As I willed my legs to straighten, all they would do was shake. I remember looking down at them and silently saying, stop shaking! They didn't listen. When I got as upright as I figured I could, I finally took my eyes off my feet to see where the ring was. My God! It looked yards away.

I was exhausted, my legs wouldn't stop shaking, and all I could think of was, I'm going to miss the ring and fall to my death! Yes, I did have a harness on that would prevent that, but my mind wasn't convinced.

I got up the courage—well, it was more like desperation to be done with this—to leap off the quivering platform and grab for the ring. Only one fingertip touched it before I found myself falling to the ground. The harness stopped me, of course, and I was fine. As they lowered me to the blessed ground beneath I imagined all those youngsters thinking, the old lady blew it. Silently, as I crawled out of the harness, I chided myself for the hysterical thoughts of doom I'd had only moments before. It was humbling to realize how little control I had over my emotions, let alone my legs! But, it was exhilarating to have faced my fear and to have done it anyway!"—Rachel J.

Like Rachel knows so well, it is easy to forget we are safe when the world looks dangerous. And when we wander from our spiritual home we often forget that we are safely tethered. We may stray from our spiritual roots, but spirit *never* leaves us. We may forget our ever-present strength, but it is always there. We only need to remember who we really are—eternal spirits playing in a fantasyland of illusion.

This world is where we learn of our true nature. Through surviving experiences of seeming danger and tragedy, we slowly remember that these challenges are here to stimulate latent memories of our spiritual being. Of all the skills we could possibly acquire to ensure a full and meaningful life, learning to manage our fearful minds is number one. Anxious self talk, doubt, worry, and distrust interfere with our ability to connect to truth. Controlling our thoughts allows us to see through their subtle deception.

We are safe. We are strong. All our frailties are products of our own imaginings. If we stop feeding these fallacies through our blind obedience to fear, they will wither. We are here to remember that we have created all we see, first through spirit, then through human endeavor. But every creation pales beside the wonder of our eternal spirit. Each is merely an illusion constructed by our unmanaged minds. In our next chapter, The Great Illusion, we will learn how to distinguish between our experiences of truth and illusion and keep our balance in a world that often confuses the two.

2   The Great Illusion

"We read the world wrong and say that it deceives us."
–Rabindranath Tagore

Author's Note: Life may appear complex and ever changing, but truth is simple and constant. Learn how truth feels and stay on your path.

Buddhism professes that enlightenment and peace come through detachment. It warns that the reality we believe we see is merely an illusion and not worthy of our devotion. It says that strong attachment to this illusion is the cause of all suffering. That to experience true peace, we need to be willing to have what we want, but be willing to not have it as well.

Detachment is a foreign concept for most of us. When we want something, we form a *strong* attachment to having it. We create a single-minded focus on achieving our desire—as our goal setting culture clearly upholds. To not have what we want is to feel that we've personally failed. We even begin to define our value by our possessions (as in *net worth*). If we have, we are worthy. If we don't have, we are deficient. If we get, we are fulfilled. If we don't get, we are empty.

We identify so strongly with the illusions of our world that we often forget that we are in this world, but not *of* it. In the world of attachment, we define ourselves by our external world experiences. But in that belief, we are ships without anchors, buffeted by whatever conditions prevail. No wonder so many people feel lost. They think they are their circumstances and possessions. They are so preoccupied by the world of illusion that they forget their eternal spirit.

We are not the *ship* on the ocean—we are the constant in a sea of change. We are the anchors—the unyielding spirit of the *I Am*. We are apart from the chaos and illusion, but also one with all that is real. This is no secret to your soul; deep within you know this. But, our human minds are often confused between illusion and reality. The two co-exist almost without distinction. What *is* real and what *is* illusion?

First, understand that illusion does not refer to the physical world's existence. A rock is hard—the air is invisible. I cannot walk through a solid wall no matter how imaginary I believe it to be. While we exist in physical bodies and judge our world with physical senses, physical objects will be real.

The illusion resides not in the physicality of our world, but in our experiences, thoughts, and attachments to what we perceive. Objects are, by definition, objective. But illusion is born of our judgments and the meaning we assign to things and events. Those meanings are simply our mind's imaginings—stories we tell ourselves to try to make sense of the life we experience.

Life may appear complex and ever changing, but truth is simple and constant. That is our clue as to what is real and what is illusion. Real *Truth*, with a capital T, never changes from day to day or person to person. But, illusion is a chameleon. It adapts and varies to suit our awareness and mood.

Truth brings clarity and union.	Illusion promotes confusion and separation.
Truth acknowledges wholeness and perfection.	Illusion causes pain and destruction.
Truth answers.	Illusion questions incessantly.
Truth reveals.	Illusion clouds and obscures.
Truth simplifies.	Illusion weaves complexity and uncertainty.
Truth shines clarifying light.	Illusion lurks in the shadows.
Truth shall set you free.	Illusion imprisons you in fear.

How can you tell if you are witnessing truth or illusion? Pay attention to your feelings. Do you feel more whole or more scattered? Are you calm or upset? Do circumstances seem simple or complex? Are you strengthened or weakened in your experience? Are love and generosity powering you or are you attacking or defending? Are you internally peaceful or does chaos rule your emotions?

Do not misunderstand, illusion can appear *very* real. And evidence and opinions may support its deception. Remember that illusion thrives in the external world. So, of course, physical evidence will align with the deception. Einstein insightfully declared that, "We can't solve problems by using the same kind of thinking we used when we created them." Your physical senses and human understanding will not help you see the illusions of our physical world. You must look with different eyes—your real eyes. Perceive from the constancy of spirit. To see truth you must come from truth.

Below, June rediscovered the truth of her partnership and herself when a wake up call shattered an easy, comfortable existence.

"Five years ago, a friend posed a pivotal question that acted like a finely targeted poison arrow piercing my heart. His question demanded that I define *life partnership*, and what I realized was I was not living the truth of my description. The pain I'd long ago buried deep within surfaced again when his question shattered the illusion of my happy life.

My emotions swung from resentment, anger, and resistance to deep enquiry, as I could no longer ignore what was so. Fourteen years of togetherness had become pleasant enough, but there was no intimate, deep connection with the one I called my partner. What had gone wrong? Could it be rectified?

I walked for hours in nature, meditating, crying, and healing years of denying this reality and the death of my dream. My mind rationalized the situation and what needed to be done and my heart was heavy with pain. But, all the while, my place of *knowing* consistently, without ever wavering, spoke the Truth.

I *knew* I needed to leave this comfortable, still loving, once passionate but now companionable relationship. I needed to be true to myself and leave the relationship. Letting go was so hard, for I had worked so diligently to rebuild my bruised life after a previous divorce. I'd re-created myself from total domesticity and motherhood to a successful professional businesswoman. To leave and face being alone and starting again seemed insurmountable.

I did leave the relationship, though it took a year to gain courage, set my mind in order and prepare my heart for what I knew would be yet more grieving. I sold my house, downsizing to live alone at a time of life when most people are starting to plan retirement. I sacked more than half my business clients, making life financially challenging, but psychologically more balanced.

I tried new, often-promised-never-done experiences to learn more about those hidden parts of myself: art, philosophy, singing, traveling, yoga, and clowning. I chose and committed to live by the creed of *does this make my heart sing*?

Four years hence, I have found a richness, happiness and serenity I never knew existed. I have less in terms of material *things*, but more of those things money just can't ever buy: love, peace, joy, and fulfillment. I have learned that giving and helping others brings more joy and love than receiving. And that happiness comes from accepting *what's* so rather than achievement of the illusion of what *might be*.

I have seen more of me than ever before, and I am very clear about who I am in the world. I live in integrity and authenticity and never compromise these core values. I am never a chameleon trying to please or win the work. I am never a victim and always take full responsibility for what I create in my world. And I have created a personal world filled with loving friends, beautiful, rich experiences that fill my soul.

Rebuilding my life has shown me that living in the flow of *trust* and *grace* brings a harmony that my planning self could never know. I set intentions rather than goals, but I'm no longer attached to their outcome. I don't need to control the process or the result. I now trust that my greater Self knows what my smaller self needs for this lifetime and it brings it to me, exactly and perfectly for the growth and experience most appropriate to my evolvement in this lifetime. Truth is always available. It lives in the knowing place within. All one ever has to do is listen and step out of the illusion." –June Hope

June abruptly woke up from her comfortable, but complacent, existence to realize how far her relationship had drifted. The reality that she'd been living was an illusion cloaking the desperation in her heart.

Don't be distracted by appearances. Look deeper—under every illusion is truth. Under the façade of happiness is often the truth of quiet desperation. Under the symptoms of your illness is the truth of your wellness. Under the harsh words from another is the truth of their fear and insecurities. And under that is the *truth* they cannot yet see for themselves: the truth of their wholeness.

Remember, truth is always simple. To master your experiences you must first learn to master your thoughts. When you feel pain, fear, separateness, and confusion—simply know that illusion is clouding the truth. Look beneath negative thoughts and feelings and seek the truth of peace. When you can separate yourself from the illusion, from the pain or confusion, you will realize the peace and wholeness beneath.

Be vigilant and you will begin to easily recognize the calling card of illusion. It always brings doubt, fear, confusion, and separation. But, these afflictions are a trick of your imagination. When first confronted by her friend, June initially felt resentment and fear. But, she looked deeper within herself and recognized that she hadn't been happy in the relationship for quite some time. She saw the illusion of her fearful emotions and chose to admit the truth. Like her, dig deeper than the surface emotions you are feeling. Deeper even than the aching heart you may feel. For beneath all the emotion is truth. Let the hurt go. Watch it lift from you and float away.

In the 1939 film, *The Wizard of Oz*, when Dorothy and her companions finally reached the Emerald City and were granted an audience with the great and powerful Wizard, he appeared as an enormous and terrifying apparition floating before them. As his voice boomed forth denial of their requests for help, Toto, Dorothy's little dog, drew back a curtain to reveal a small and timid man running a machine that projected a Wizard that was only an illusion.

Illusion can appear convincing and even intimidating, like the Wizard. But, it is an apparition made of imagined fears and unmanaged emotions. Challenge its validity and when the veil is parted, you will see the truth that was always there. You are eternal. You are safe. You are stronger than anything this world visits upon you.

In Personal Inventories, our next chapter, looking at truth and illusion in our own attitudes and beliefs will give us a chance to make some serious decisions about where we aren't living up to our own truths.

3 Personal Inventories

*"The chains of habits are too weak to be felt
until they are too strong to be broken."*
-Samuel Johnson (1709-1784)

*Author's Note: Overcome limiting habits and make easy, small steps that add up to
huge wins every time.*

E ach year businesses take inventory of the stock in their stores and warehouses. They organize and count each widget and thingamabob to see what they have and what might need to be ordered or even discarded. You have probably seen them, employees with hand held electronic scanners and clipboards of product descriptions picking up and counting each and every item on the shelf. It is a painstaking process requiring a sharp eye and complete focus. And, in the end, the business knows exactly what it does and does not have on hand.

Perhaps we should borrow this practice to attend to our own inventories. How useful would it be to take stock of those habits and perceptions that constitute your own personal *being* inventory? To know what in your *warehouse* is overstocked and what is almost depleted. To toss out habits and perceptions that no longer serve you. To order up experiences and results that have been on back order for longer than you can remember.

Grab a piece of paper, we are going to do some work here. Go ahead . . . I will wait.

Okay, now down the left side of the page, with a few inches of writing space between them, copy down these headings:

1. Destructive Habits
2. Stinky Attitudes
3. Beliefs That Get Me Into Trouble
4. Neglected Relationships
5. Forgotten Dreams
6. Numbed-out Feelings
7. Flabby Health
8. Lost Ambition

Quite a list! It is inevitable that those neglected corners of our lives accumulate dust and debris when we are not looking.

Take a few minutes to consider your inventory for each category. What habits have you unsuccessfully tried to change? What attitudes are poisoning your days? What condition is your body in? What relationship have you all but forgotten? Take a good hard look. This inventory is what gives your life the color it has. It molds your experiences.

It creates your future.

Taking inventory periodically gives us a chance to clean house, discard the old us that we have outgrown, and evolve all our natures. That can mean the difference between just being alive or really LIVING!

Mary Anne learned this lesson after years of self-sabotage and heartache.

"I was raised by wonderful parents—parents who *never* fought. But, when I was 13-years-old, my parents came out of the bedroom and told us kids they were getting a divorce. I was only three years old at the time. I was devastated.

For the next fifteen years or so, I had trust issues, including self-sabotage and I felt like I was damaged goods. The root of my problems— I didn't trust my instincts because how could I *not* see my parent's divorce coming? So anytime I was in a relationship and it was going very well, I waited for the bottom to drop out. If the bottom didn't drop out, I would see to it that it did.

Until finally, the most incredible man in the world came into my life. He was patient with me, kind, loving and sent from above. After several lumps, I cleaned up my act and decided to live each day to the fullest and be the best person I can be. We've been married two years today. Since I stopped believing that the worst always happens, my life has been full of love, joy, peace, kindness, and goodness."

–Mary Anne Butz-Belanger

Like Mary Anne, we have each learned, through our own hard lessons, that without internal changes, our external life stays about the same. Why is it then that we expect to live a more fulfilling life tomorrow when we keep doing what we have done for the last countless years? For things to change, *you* have got to change! Today! Now! Start doing something different—even a small step.

I know a small step does not seem to change much *out* there. But, it is a huge step inside. Just by driving to work a different way sends a message to your brain that "something is different." And when one thing is different, you can break the mindless routine of old habits. You will wake up and begin to notice life again. One little change creates just enough momentum to make it possible for other, perhaps more important things to begin to change too.

You see, there is no order of difficulty in change. A big change is no more difficult than a small one. Because change isn't about the thing you're trying to change. Change is about a decision. It is making a different choice . . . inviting other possibilities . . . thinking differently.

And here is where it gets even better. Small changes can lead to *huge* outcomes! Why? Because the momentum of life is cumulative. Each day builds on the previous. Like a drop in the bucket that holds the totality of your life. Each drop, each day, seems almost inconsequential. But, with each drop, the bucket slowly fills and suddenly, as if in an instant, it overflows and life shifts.

"I think once you start making some changes and deciding on your direction, you just start rolling with it. The hardest thing is making the decision. But once you make the decision, you just keep going. The process just rolls and you realize the decisions you make from that decision are ok." –Marcie L.

There is an ancient Chinese tale that illustrates this point. In a serene rural pond a lily seed fell from a passing bird. It sprouted and blossomed into a beautiful white flower. No one witnessed the lone lily floating in the large pond. The next day the lily produced a second flower. Now two pads lay on the water. Still no one noticed the lilies. The following day the two lilies became four. No one noticed.

Each day the lilies doubled until one day, someone *did* notice. The lovely flowers had covered almost half the pond. Who could imagine the destruction they could cause? An alarmed villager did and warned his neighbors that something should be done. If the lilies covered *the pond's entire surface*, the fish below would die from lack of oxygen, and the fish were the main diet of the local villagers. The villagers vowed to meet the next day to discuss what to do. But, you guessed it . . . the next morning the whole pond was covered with lilies, and dead fish lined the banks.

Your life is like that pond. Each day a lily blooms and shapes the future of your existence. Lilies like neglect, procrastination, busy-ness, excuses, and waste. One lily of neglect does not seem to make much difference. Not telling your child how much you believe in her today surely will not destroy her self-esteem. But, years of neglecting to say that you are proud of her or believe in her can ruin a relationship—and perhaps even a life.

One drop in the bucket, one lily on the pond, or one choice can seem inconsequential at the time. It is easy to overlook the far-reaching impact of a simple misstep. Yet, it is in that failure to notice that we surrender control of our lives.

Go back to the personal inventory list you started earlier and consider where you are in life. What destructive habits do you have? Does smoking one cigarette kill you? Does telling a little white lie matter? How about 10,000 cigarettes? Deceiving the one you love?

And what of your neglected dreams? What does it matter that you got too busy today to plan for that dream trip to Alaska; to study French; to sign up for college; to call your mom? Missing one day cannot mean that much! Right? Probably not . . . there will always be tomorrow.

But, here is what *does* matter: you caved in to neglect today. And it will be easier to do the same thing again tomorrow. And pretty soon tomorrow is next decade and putting it off becomes an unconscious habit. Procrastination and neglect are like mosquitoes. They anesthetize you while they suck your life dry.

Take stock of your personal inventory of habits, attitudes, and choices that gradually set the tone of your life. Look closely at the lilies covering your pond. Ignoring them is not wise. They are already shaping the quality and direction of your future. Ignorance is not bliss! Ignorance can be suicide. Choose to sort through your inventory and discard that which is destroying your dreams or your life. *Know* your inventory well. Only then can you do something about it. It may not be pleasant, but do it any way. It will be your ammunition against wasted opportunities to live an extraordinary life.

> "I'm a very positive and upbeat person. I encourage other people when they get down. But, I can see that I'm not practicing my own preaching because I get very discouraged myself. What you wrote showed me that I've got to start tending to my own garden." –Kathy Hageman

Buried deep within many peoples' inventories—stuck way back on a high shelf—is one habit that can ruin lives. It's the habit of asking disempowering questions. You know, those questions you ask yourself that make you feel victimized and unworthy.

In the next chapter, we'll take a look at the deadliest question of all, and with an almost imperceptible correction, you'll purge yourself forever of this life debilitating adversary.

4 The Power of the Question

"Have patience with everything that remains unsolved in your heart.
Try to love the questions themselves, like locked rooms and like books
written in a foreign language. Do not now look for the answers.
They cannot now be given to you because you could not live them.
It is a question of experiencing everything.
At present you need to live the question.
Perhaps you will gradually, without even noticing it, find yourself
experiencing the answer, some distant day."
—Rainer Maria Rilke, Letters to a Young Poet

Author's Note: Looking for answers? The quality of the question you ask determines the richness of the answer you're capable of hearing.

Who are you and why are you here? For many, these questions are yet unanswered. And unanswered questions of this magnitude often create discomfort and confusion. The answers can take years of simmering before we are clear. To deal with the persistent anxiety of not knowing such essential answers, we sometimes reach for the instant relief of a quick answer. Not primarily to find the *right* answer, but to end the discomfort of confusion.. Unanswered questions threaten our finely groomed realities. Especially questions of true importance, like the purpose of our lives, or who we really are. When confused or uncertain, we tend to seek the relief of a quick answer. Not particularly for the sake of finding the right answer, but to end the discomfort of not knowing. We'll do almost anything to get out of the purgatory of the unknown.

But, momentous questions like these do not come with tidy answers. Fundamental life questions like 1) where did I come from? 2) who am I? or 3) what's my purpose? require room to breathe and develop. They herald transformational life changes that draw a line between your past and your future—where life irreversibly shifts. This is not the time to hurry or get impatient. Much is at stake.

Before habitually seeking comfort, perhaps we should explore the value of *purposeful* discomfort. If you can be with the question and not resist its inherent murkiness, then you might gain the clarity to truly understand the question that life is asking of you before you rush to an answer.

One of the questions that cause us the most anguish is a question to which there is often no satisfactory answer. It's the most prevalent question we utter when we are hurt or wronged. "Why is this happening to me?" This heart wrenching plea does not really seek an answer; it mostly wants justification.

You may have muttered it before. Hoping for whatever *this* represents to stop. "Why is this happening to me?" is often unanswerable, and even if answered, provides little relief. Asking this question only serves to reinforce our status as victim. It leaves us feeling hopeless, indignant, judgmental, or even angry. These are not the most empowering feelings, are they?

But, there *is* a question at moments like this, which does have a real possibility of being answered. All it requires is a small modification to the wording. Rather than asking, "Why is this happening to me?" instead ask, "Why is this happening for me?"

Notice how you physically feel when you change that one little word. Lighter. Attentive. Your focus moves from judgment and resistance to curiosity and exploration. You begin to look at circumstances with an inquisitive eye. You examine, not resist. Changing one word has changed your entire relationship with the unknown. And it has brought you strength, not fed your fear. A reader discovered this very fact.

> "I've gotten feedback from a mentor that I don't speak up in meetings, and he knows that I have a lot more to offer. My response was, 'I'm usually thinking about how to articulate my thoughts without sounding like an idiot.' Of course, this means that sometimes the opportunity to make a comment passes and I wind up swallowing my words. We had to laugh because he's also Asian and understands the culture, but he told me that when he forced himself to speak up, even at the risk of sounding like a jerk, he was more successful in his career. So, lesson learned . . . instead of thinking, *Why don't I speak up more*? A simple shift in the questions I ask myself can change the way I handle a situation. Instead of focusing on the past, by asking why, I can focus on the future by asking how. I get to ask myself, 'How can I speak up more?'" –A. O.

The quality of the question you ask yourself is inseparably linked to the richness of the answer available to you. Read these questions to yourself and notice how each makes you feel.

Why am I unhappy? or How can I become happy?

Why don't I know my purpose? or How can I become aware of my purpose?

Why am I so poor? or How can I make more money?

Why don't they understand me? or How can I be better understood?

Notice that each of the *why* questions above reflects a current condition. But, that current reality is, in truth, a result of the past. "Why am I unhappy?" is a question you ask now, but it is based upon all that has led up to the now. You did not suddenly become unhappy this moment. Unhappiness has probably been building for a long time. *Why* questions keep you focused on the past. They keep you stuck in the unhappiness, not exploring a way out.

When you stop asking *why* and begin to ask *how*, you will move toward new possibilities and solutions. You won't agonize over what is already irreversibly done. You cannot change the past, no matter how much you want to. You can only change the present and, therefore, the future.

"When you said to stop asking why something bad is happening TO me and ask why it's happening FOR me, a very, very, very large BONG went off in my head. It was a life changing statement. I was so into 'WHY ME?' that when the bong sounded, my whole body SHOOK as if an earthquake were occurring. Thank you for the opportunity to be released from THAT bondage. You are wonderful."

—Barbara Reynolds

Why is often a rhetorical question that merely keeps you locked in an endless loop. Explaining the past does not move you toward real solutions. It just conjures up possible justifications for your predicament. Unfortunately, none of those reasons, even when known, are likely to make you any happier.

How questions lead toward possible change in the situation. They ask your brain to think of options and solutions. They focus you on what you can do *now* to change the situation.

One of my "Waking Up" readers faced a situation that could have easily made her a victim, had she focused on *why*. Instead, she chose to take control and employed a more powerful how to deal with her dilemma. This is her story.

"I come from a logic oriented family. Both of my parents were computer pioneers. Mathematics was always my favorite subject in school because there was one right answer and you could prove it. I wasn't really exposed to any 'spirituality' growing up, so I never understood the concepts of faith or trusting your gut. What was real for me was something I could see and touch.

I followed in my parents' footsteps and got my college degree in Computer Science. I began my professional life as a systems programmer, then a software developer, then a technical trainer, and finally a technical marketer. Each job was progressively less logic oriented. I began to embrace faith in a reality I couldn't see, prove, or touch. My life experiences were shaping me to see that there was more to life than accepting only what I could prove.

About this time 'Waking Up' also became a perfect element in my personal growth. I can see how instrumental it has been in shaping my character and preparing me for the next phase of my life. I liken 'Waking Up' to my character work out. On a weekly basis I've been challenged to look at life differently and to continually grow. I'm still logical, but now I pause during a life experience and reflect on it rather than just accepting it or not even noticing it. I now truly experience and direct my life.

I've recently left my job of 18 years to mother our daughters full-time. We also moved 1,200 miles from the area I lived in for 40 years to a place where I know no one. Once we were unpacked in our new home, we had hundreds of cardboard boxes on our front porch. My kids asked why we didn't just throw them away. I explained to them about recycling and how each of us can make a difference to save our environment.

Unfortunately, we moved to an area that isn't very environmentally conscious. A year ago I would have gotten very disappointed with this town's lack of vision, and I would have just put those boxes out for the trash. Instead, I spent hours finding a place that recycles cardboard. My children and I drove 20 minutes to the recycling drop and unloaded all of the cardboard boxes.

All the while, I was cognizant of the fact that my kids were watching me, but also being taught by what I value. Those were the best few hours of my life! I've gone on now to start recycling centers here in Colorado. I contacted a recycling company who was willing to set up their recycle bins. They'll even pay $10.00 towards a charity for every time they get it picked up. I contacted a gal this morning about her local charity here. If we set up 20 drop off stations in the area, we believe we can get about $500 a month for her charity!

Just the other day, my six year old gave me a birthday card that said, 'Thank you for your help in saving our environment.' I was so touched to know my daughter had been so profoundly affected by how I'd dealt with an obstacle thrown in my path. Now I will forever be grateful for that obstacle and how my response reflected so positively on someone I love.

You've told us before that our thoughts and actions define who we become. I just absolutely loved that! Now I think of that every day. Everything I come across, every thought that I'm thinking, seeing, doing; I'm just defining who I am! It's extremely self empowering. And it makes me realize that my effort to live according to my ethics and to recycle those cardboard boxes also showed my children who I am.

Parents are such important role models to their kids. It's not what we say, but what we do that makes the biggest impression. Recycling was my thing, but I included my kids in something that was important to me by talking about it and sharing the opportunity with them to participate in it with me. I think in focusing on how my decisions form who I am, I'm also teaching my children how to be ethical and responsible adults. Rather than complain about what isn't, I hope I'm showing them how to be the change they want to see—to take responsibility for what they believe in and to show the world who they are."—Sue Hoffman

Pay close attention to the type of questions you ask when you are disappointed by life and when your expectations are not met. When you catch yourself asking *why*, immediately transform the question into a more powerful opportunity for discovery. Make achieving what you desire a higher priority than your need to be right about your past.

Once, after listening to me endlessly grumble about how I had *been wronged*, a friend asked me, "Would you rather be right or happy?" Of course, I answered that I wanted to be right! It took me a few days to appreciate the full weight of his question. My need to have my way was making me miserable. I was choosing to righteously wallow in my indignation about what *should* be, instead of dealing with my reality. His question let me see that my happiness and peace were more important than a past I could not change.

As you find yourself asking why questions, notice where you may be choosing to have your way at the price of having your peace. *Why* will perpetuate upset; *how* will end it. This is not about giving up or giving in, it is about prioritizing your happiness. What is it that you really want? What choice right now would best achieve happiness? Is this momentary issue more important than your sanity and peace?

Now, choose again. Choose sanity, not resentment. Choose possibility, not regret, even in the face of devastation. Because when all about you is falling apart, even then, you can choose your experience. Will you choose to let suffering impair your ability to move forward? Or will you ask a different question about what it all means? None of us relishes starting over, but new beginnings bring new possibilities and new growth, as we'll see in the next chapter.

5   Start Again

"The world is round and the place which may seem like the end
may also be the beginning."
--Ivy Baker Priest

Author's Note: When the dream dies, regain your footing and soar even higher.

Starting over is the moment when one thing ends and another begins; two moments in one reality; the alpha and omega that engender such a confusion of feelings of disappointment, gratitude, fear, and defiance. To a stunning degree, the quality of your life depends upon how you handle the emotional turbulence of a closing door and in which direction you find yourself facing. As in every part of life, it is not what happens to you that determines your fate. It is what you do next.

We each have our own stories—many of them. Those heart-stopping moments when we realized that a dream was not going to come true. When we held shattered plans in our hands and could not make it better. With eyes cast to the ground, it was then that we answered the question we must all face at times like these.

How do I deal with this?

Will I be bitter that I was cheated of my chance? Will I scream to the top of my blistered lungs that it is not fair? Will I envy and begrudge those who have received what *I deserved*? Will I antacid my rancor and inebriate my rage? Will I clothe myself in resentment and withdraw from life; or bed-down in the arms of self-pity?

Or will I turn my anger inward and condemn myself for not being good enough? Slink back into the land of self-pitying mediocrity where no one expects much of me anyway? Will I lick my wounds and beseech sympathy from other co-dependent could-have-beens? Will I dare not look up from my shoes for fear of being hurt again? Will I pine in silence for a life I will never have?

Hopefully, I will remember that every door has two sides and that, opened or closed, it is a temporary orientation. Will I remember that it is through resolve that life-forces awaken the primal substance of my dreams? Will I remember that comfort is not a sign of success and unquestioned answers are meaningless?

Life is not in the answer business. It, forever and always, asks questions. And the questions all have the same root. Who are you becoming? Who will you create yourself to be? What will you choose to do with your talents? Will your presence linger in this world once you have gone? How will you deal with defeat? What purpose will consume you—heart and soul?

Life will undoubtedly deliver your fair share of pain and setbacks. And that's not necessarily bad. Hardship is the stone on which we are honed into stronger humans and higher expressions of spirit. It is through our difficulties that we learn patience and humility and compassion. To wish for a life of ease and comfort is pointless. Life is not easy or comfortable. Life just *is*. Struggle or ease, comfort or pain, are merely judgments we make about our experience. It is not what happens that determines your fate. It is what you do next.

Every day you discover who you are. You bump up against life and determine how you'll respond. And it's in that very response that you forge your character and your fate. It's best you pay more attention to your response than to the event to which you are reacting. The event is just the event. It has no inherent meaning. It is simply an opportunity for self-discovery and choice.

> "I'm embarking on a new journey and anything is possible if I don't let the fears get the best of me. The fears of the unknown will always be with me: fear of failure, fear of new experiences, fear of meeting new people, fear of leaving my comfortable space and venturing forth into the world where I am vulnerable and may make mistakes. But it's okay to make mistakes. Your words have shown me that it is human to question ourselves and change our minds. No one is perfect.
>
> Even at the age of fifty-eight, it's okay to start over. In fact, it is more than okay; it is an imperative for me. I had grown tired of the corporate world and my job. I wasn't excited or inspired anymore. The company's aspirations and goals were not important to me anymore. My life, my goals and my values are important and I'm working toward attaining goals that will enrich my life while still representing my values." –Jennifer Robins

When life gets hard and your world crumbles, ask, "Who will I be now?" With each response to setbacks ask, "Who am I becoming with this choice?"

Every choice and decision you make defines who you are. It reveals your internal thoughts, fears, and ambitions. Each day you write your autobiography one page at a time. You script your life and the script reveals who you are. Is your demonstration of who you are reflecting who you want to be? You might say that you value your family above all else, but how do you treat them? Do you spend time with them? Are they at the top of your priority list? Your actions speak more truthfully than your words.

Your *real* values are reflected in your choices. And your choices reflect who you are. If you want to really know someone well, stop listening to who they say they are and just watch their choices. You will learn much and quickly.

If you are not happy with your reflection, only you can change it. If you are not happy with who you have become, make a vow to make different choices, choices that the person you would like to become would make. Be an actor. Behave yourself into becoming the person you wish to be. Choose differently, and with each conscious choice you will create yourself anew.

Dennis found his world shattered and questioned who he was when a door closed. He was forced to rediscover his sense of self and find a way to move forward in peace.

"You told us, 'Through all thoughts and deeds, you're defining yourself.' I think of that every day. It's extremely self-empowering. I'm not a victim of what comes at me. I participate and create the life I want. This has made all the difference in how I'm raising my children."
—Sue Hoffman

"As I write this note it's August, and I'm on vacation with my two sons, thirteen and eleven, and my lovely daughter, age ten. This time is precious because I can fully enjoy them, and they get ALL of me. I disappeared for three and a half years until I started my life over again on January 3rd.

I had just completed another let's-keep-it-together-for-the-kids'-Christmas. It had actually gone very well. On January 3rd, I again saw my attorney who said the divorce would be final January 13th, unless I wasn't ready. Right then it hit me. I'm ready. It's time to get on with my life, no longer letting things happen to me, but starting a new life outside of what I'd known for eighteen years of marriage. I moved out three days later. It was one of the toughest things I've ever done, but everyone, including the kids, knew it was the right thing to do.

Looking back, I am still not sure how or why it happened. My mid forties wife of fifteen years, who I adored, told me she loved me, but was not in love with me. It was a shot to the head, the stomach, and my ego. I spent a long time trying to be the person she might love. What did I need to change so she would love me? I needed my fairytale life of a beautiful wife, my three beautiful children, a good job, and a good home to be mine again.

I invested too much of the next three years letting how someone else felt about me determine my self-worth. Eventually I realized this was not about me. I was consumed with this to a degree that pieces of me were growing dormant. I had a single focus, avoiding what was inevitable—my divorce. I was not whole to anyone, my kids, family, friends, or to my work. In time I realized it wasn't my wife I was hesitant to divorce, it was my life. Not being able to kiss my kids good night or goodbye before school was going to be tough. But the issues to be solved were out of my control and it was time to move on.

When I left the house that day in January I vowed not to dwell on how we/I got to where we were. Looking forward is what would keep my resolve and bring me back. Is it easy? NO. Within two months my mom died suddenly, and I had to put my dog of fourteen years down. Within sixty days I had lost my wife, my house, my mom, and my dog. Even though these may be great musings for a country music song, they're tough emotions to live through.

I survived it all and continue to move forward because I chose to start again. I have bad memories, and some emotional scars. Some days I feel like I died, and my exwife and kids are moving on without me. I recently flew back from New York to home, got off the plane and realized there was nobody to go home to. I do not expect to float into the future. I'll have setbacks, though they can be self-correcting with enough determination.

But because I have chosen to take control, I am more self-aware and able to understand my emotions and continue to move on to the next phase in my life. I'm BACK, because I choose to make the rest of my life happen, not happen to me.

While going through all of this, I read Karen's e-zine regularly. I was on such a hunt for answers, many of which did not exist. I even read all of the Dr. Phil books, though they basically say the same stuff in different formats. You did this work, your passion to reach and help others find answers. I don't have them all, but I do appreciate your insights."—Dennis J.

Even in the hardest challenges you face, life *wants* you to succeed. It is not out to defeat you. Life wants you to be spectacular. It has never once told you "No." Certainly, you may have *heard* "No," but it emanated from your own mind. And, ironically, what you heard was not "No," it was "Know." It was the holiest of wisdoms calling you to remember the Truth of who you are.

When your head is filled with the myth of defeat, remember that nothing is denied you. We don't always know the path we will live. Like children who don't know what's best for them, we are also sometimes blind to the way that will bring us our greatest good. Know that every event, appearing good or bad, is specifically designed to bring you wholeness. Know your power.

In each instance of your past, when it felt like all was falling apart, haven't you now recognized the growth and strength you found from having had that experience? Our lessons are often brought to us cloaked in the disguise of its opposite. We learn to let go by hanging on too tight. We learn to heal when we've been weary with grief. The lessons can be hard, but they are not purposeless. Starting again means believing that there is a light ahead, even if we cannot yet see it.

Whatever difficult moment you are now experiencing, choose to start again. Choose to *know* now. You can. Choice *is* the door to the answer you seek. And that door will open to endless others. How do you choose to create your life? Choose that and know the Truth.

Perhaps our biggest challenge walking through life, with all the joys and disappointments, is discovering who we really are and remaining true to ourselves always. In the next chapter, Forever and Always Me, we'll consider how we might, even unconsciously, be compromising our integrity to win the approval of others.

6 Forever and Always Me

"The individual has always had to struggle to keep from being overwhelmed by the tribe. If you try it, you will be lonely often, and sometimes frightened. But no price is too high to pay for the privilege of owning yourself."
–Friedrich Nietzsche

Author's Note: The greatest satisfaction in life is being who you really are in every moment. Why is it that that level of honesty scares us so?

It is said that when we come into this world we forget that we are spiritually whole and eternal. We don the garb of a physical body and start with a clean slate to begin the process of remembering who we really are. In our early years, we grow at a mentally astounding rate—more than we ever will again. We learn laws of physics, mostly by falling down and other such run-ins with the physical realities of life. We learn language and the skill of communicating. We focus on the external world to gather in as much information and experience as we can, so that we can learn to be in this world.

But, the real question is, what is it that we learn to be? Throughout our childhood and well into early adulthood, we often *make* ourselves from the opinions and feedback we get from those around us. Dad tells his little son that he is so strong. And the child purposefully finds ways to use his muscles to impress others and receive praise. He exercises to make his strength even more noticeable. He might test himself against others or get involved in sports. Because he believes Dad's words, he makes them part of who he believes he is.

But, not all opinions we hear about us are positive. A young girl criticizes her classmate by telling her that she's not pretty, and the classmate closes down a little. Unsure of herself, the classmate hesitates to seek out romantic friendships; she dresses so as to not be noticed; she seeks the company of others she deems aren't that great looking either to feel like she belongs. When someone really *is* attracted to her, she assumes they are feeling sorry for her or are trying to humiliate her, and she refuses their affections.

Throughout our lives we take in opinions from people about who we are and what we can do. We use that feedback to construct ourselves into a person who either fits that description, or perhaps rebels against it altogether. Either way, to a large degree, we use input from the outside world to create our lives and ourselves.

We try to meet expectations; especially those expectations from the people we care for most. We may marry someone we aren't really in love with just to avoid hurting their feelings, because we can't bring ourselves to tell them the truth. We may study for a career in college that doesn't really appeal to us to fulfill a parent's dream. We too often play the game set before us, pleasing the ones whose love and acceptance we most need.

I listened to a young woman a few years back talk of her fear that the man she loved might leave her. Joyce had done everything she could to make him happy. She'd changed her hair and lost weight. She'd gone back to school to learn a more respectable career than what he deemed she was in. She'd ignored her friends and the activities she used to love to do, so that she could be with him and be part of his interests.

It was clear that Joyce was not only miserable, but she was also afraid. She wanted this relationship so badly that she'd do just about anything to keep it. Including masking her own needs and giving up her own dreams.

After listening to her anguish over not being able to please her man, I asked her, "What if you did make one more change, whatever it might be, and he suddenly showered you with affection and devotion? Would that make you happy?"

She didn't even hesitate long enough for me to finish my question before she blurted out, "Yes! That's what I dream of!"

I'd assumed as much and asked, "But who would he be loving?" From the look on her face, I could tell she didn't understand. "After all the things you've changed about yourself to earn his love, would he be loving *you* or the fantasy you've created to match his desires? If he did fall in love with this creation of yours, wouldn't you always know that he loved the image you created, and not you? Could you live with that?"

We sat silently for a few minutes as she came to see that her strategy for getting him to love her was only getting him to love an illusion, and not her. Joyce had thrown aside all the things that were who she was. *She* was no longer in this relationship. It was all a lie.

As social creatures by nature, we all have a strong desire to fit in to be wanted and appreciated; to belong is our dream. We fail to understand that, in belonging, union and diversity must coexist. We fear that being different will bring rejection. But, we are all different from one another. We are all unique. Belonging doesn't mean uniformity. We don't have to sacrifice ourselves to have a place in this world.

The people we often find it most difficult to be truthful with are family members. This young reader is struggling through her teen years to find out who she is, aside from who her family believes she should be.

"Strained and distant, my dad and I have always had a somewhat awkward relationship. For whatever reason, we didn't see eye to eye on how to live life. He couldn't understand how I was content to watch instead of being in the moment, and he frequently told me with a sneer to 'get a life.' Hurt and more than a little confused, I'd fire back with, 'What do you think I'm living?'

But inside I constantly thought there was something about me that didn't quite add up. I began to feel ashamed that I was scared to put myself out there, and I only made matters worse when I would attempt to be more outgoing. It wasn't me and my privacy wasn't something I *wanted* to change. Instead, I decided to hide it from him; easy enough to do since his job took him out of town most of the time. I kept telling myself he would love me more if he thought I'd gotten past my shyness, even if I hadn't really changed at all.

Pleasing him became more important to me than how I felt about myself. For a while I was convinced that he knew what was best in terms of my personality. 'I'm proud of you, Hon, for facing that challenge,' he'd say. My face lit up every time he praised me. But, deep inside, I knew I was misleading him. I was caught between being myself and being a *good daughter*. I'd think *it's good that you're changing. You want him to love you, don't you?* Of course I did, but a question in the back of my mind kept trying to surface. *Does he love the real you?*

Pretending to be someone I wasn't began to wear me down. Being around my dad caused me to be wary and . . . uncomfortable. I was two people; I no longer knew who I was. Feeling alone, I drew into myself and shut everything—and everyone—out. My hours after school were spent alone in my room, where I worked on my assignments and read.

One night, late, my dad and I had a good heart-to-heart. At least he thought so; I wasn't so sure myself. We discussed my responsibilities, changes in my life, etc. Although I heard him speaking, I noticed his criticism the most. When I'd tell him about what happened at school, he'd point out my mistakes. Then I'd have to listen to him lecture as he all but disregarded the fact I handled everything fine.

I had mixed emotions after that. It angered me, and then hurt that he wouldn't acknowledge the good in me. All he did was focus on my flaws. I wanted to tell him how I felt, and even tried to. Sadly, he didn't want to hear me. I knew in that moment I had to find myself or continue holding on to a love that wasn't mine at all.

Finding myself wasn't difficult, but full of uncertainties. Letting go of who I thought I should've been was gut wrenching. It was like a dying man cutting off the very hold he had of life. Some nights in bed I'd cry for the hopelessness of the situation. What was I hoping to gain from this? Independence? I wasn't sure that risking my dad's love was smart. Other days I couldn't have been in better spirits. One of my best friends complimented me once by saying, 'You're really fun to be around. We've missed you.'

To this day, I take time out for me. My dad and I aren't as close as before, my single regret in this lesson. I know now that it's important to be yourself, especially when it comes to love and being loved. Our greatest strength and gift wouldn't be as special without the courage to give it to ourselves freely."—Reader

Even at a very young age, this teen felt the dilemma we all experience at some point in our lives. One day we look in the mirror at the lives we've woven around us and emptiness hits us full force. Where did we go? How did all this come about, when it isn't what we really wanted or who we really are? It's a jarring awakening to have a life, but not be in it.

What makes you *you*? What are your unique perspectives and individual talents? Do you hide them or contribute them to the developing tapestry of your world? If those around you are of one opinion, but you see it differently, do you keep quiet to maintain your position in the group? Or do you offer your differing view so that others may see new possibilities?

Each one of us reaches a point in our lives when who we are and what others want us to be are incongruent. And we recognize that to not be true to ourselves is to throw away our very lives. This is the moment we really grow up and stop solicitously seeking approval. That's when we can break free of often self-imposed limitations and gift the world with the special talents that only we can give.

We each have a gift to give this world—a part to play in its and our unfolding. In the following chapter, A Simple Thank You, we'll re-experience the importance of recognizing others for their gifts and the profound difference that doing so can make in the life of another.

7 A Simple Thank You

"There is more hunger for love and appreciation in this world than for bread." –Mother Teresa

Author's Note: Want to make a difference? Use these two simple words to transform you and the world.

I did it again this week. And it felt so good I wondered why I didn't do it every day. It was simple really . . . no bother or fuss. But, from the reaction I got, you would have thought I'd done something really incredible. I said, "Thank you." Not to my client or my friend . . . not to my mom or neighbor. I said it to a total stranger. Why? Because they deserved it and I wanted them to know that they had made a difference in my world.

Two weeks ago I drove to the Mirabeau Point entrance of The Centennial Trail that extends thirty-nine miles from Spokane, Washington, east into Idaho, through Coeur d'Alene and beyond. The trailhead is close to my home and I enjoy the peaceful and spectacularly beautiful walk along the fir lined, westward flowing Spokane River.

When I arrived, the large parking lot was already filled with the cars and SUVs of other like-minded walkers, runners, rollerbladers, and bikers looking for a day's adventure and camaraderie. As busy as the trail can get, I had heard of a few car break-ins and vandalism at some of the trailheads, so I always locked my car and prayed I would return to find it undisturbed.

This particular morning, upon my return to the parking lot, I saw a security car parked beside my vehicle. An officer in a denim-blue uniform sat on his car's front fender gazing peacefully at the easy-flowing river below.

Just seeing him there made me feel a bit safer. I opened my car door to get in and then hesitated. I was grateful for this gentleman's presence and vigilance and I thought, why not tell him so?

My approach broke his reverie and he looked in my direction startled and momentarily disoriented. His expression turned a bit wary as he spun to face me head-on. I met his uneasy gaze with a big smile and without hesitation said, "I just want you to know that I am really glad you are here and watching out for us."

His caution evaporated in the radiance of his huge smile. He literally beamed at me as he proudly announced that there had been *no* car break-ins at *his* lot in the last five months and only one close call.

Like the river flowing below, his words gushed freely as he told me in great detail about the excitement of the day before. When he had arrived at the trail entrance, he had spotted a coat floating at the river's edge. He thought it was probably left by a kid the day before or perhaps lost by one of the many kayakers that regularly challenge the river. After surveying the immediate area around the coat, he saw no reason for concern, so he picked it up to take to the parks department's lost and found.

As he climbed back up the hill to the parking lot, he noticed an older teenage boy trying to jimmy a car lock. When he noticed the officer, the kid was pretty cool as he pretended that the car was his and that he had locked his keys inside. But the officer had seen the lady who owned the car park it there about twenty minutes before. The officer figured the Walkman, sitting clear as day on the passenger seat, had caught the boy's attention. *Will people ever learn*, he wondered.

It was evident, from the live-action telling of this incident, that the officer really liked his job and felt responsible for the safety of the visitors to *his* trail. The kid had done no damage to the car and the officer figured that the owner would probably never know he had foiled a robbery. But, he said, he didn't need praise; he just wanted to do his job well.

I wished him a good day and returned to my car. He waved robustly as I drove off. I watched him in my rearview mirror until I could no longer see him. He never stopped waving. His gratitude made me feel as though I had just presented him with a medal of valor. I choked up a bit wondering when he had last heard someone thank him for doing his job. Probably a long time. Maybe never.

A few weeks later, at the same trailhead, I came upon two women mowing and cleaning the picnic area by the waterfall. The day was beautiful and the air smelled sweetly of freshly cut grass. My experience with the officer had made me feel so good that I decided I would thank these ladies for their work, too. But, before I could reach them, they got in their truck and drove off. I was so disappointed.

But . . . as I walked back to my car, there they were! They had driven over to have breakfast on a bench by the river. When I approached, they kept talking and paid me no mind. I stood for a moment and then gently interrupted, "Thank you for the work you do. Everything looks so beautiful."

There was that smile! Ear to ear . . . both of them. The *stranger* in them vanished and they told me that this was their last week of work. Summer was over and we, who enjoy the trail, would have to fend for

> "I love to tip the people serving me at the drive-in window. They're ALWAYS shocked and pleasantly surprised to be appreciated. I feel that they're working as hard as the people who wait on us at tables inside!"
>
> –Dora-Faye Hendricks

ourselves until next year. They chimed in that they would miss their jobs. And their glowing expressions proved their sincerity.

As I got in my car to drive home, I felt an odd mix of gratitude and sadness. I was grateful that I had taken a moment in my day to thank a stranger for making the quality of my life better. And I was sad to think of all the dedicated public workers out there who never hear how appreciated they are. It takes so little to give . . . just a thought; just a moment. But, thank you can be the most precious words a person hears all day. And people always receive it with surprise and a moment of inner recognition that they do make a difference.

Whether surprising an unsuspecting person with a word of thanks, or reaching out to someone desperate for a touch of human kindness, you have the power to change lives—including your own.

Give yourself a beautiful gift today by letting someone, who will not expect it, know that you appreciate what s/he does to make your life better. Let her know that her life matters. You won't have to look far. They are everywhere: the bag boy at the grocery store who happily takes your bags to your car in the pouring rain; the crossing guard at the school who puts her own life between your children and danger everyday; and the janitor wiping down the tables in the food court at the mall. When do you think s/he last heard thank you?

Many people serve us every day. Some we never see. They take on jobs doing what many of us would not want to do, but jobs that need doing just the same. They serve and are, more often than not, ignored by those they serve.

The status and hierarchy we maneuver within each day will, one day, mean absolutely nothing. We are all just people with the same dreams and needs as everyone else. And supreme of all these is the need to be appreciated and to know that we personally make a difference and that our lives matter.

Tell someone you do not know how much you appreciate his or her work. The smile you will get will make your day! And you may become as addicted to this as I have become. Wouldn't it be something if everyone thanked just one person everyday for his or her contribution? Imagine the smiles . . . now that would be a wonderful world!

In the chapters of Act One: The Cone Awaits, we focus on who you are and how you demonstrate that you to the world. These include the self-identities we create in this world. In the Act Two: The Fires Come: sharpening your spiritual skills, we'll dig into how each of us learns to navigate our life's journey through knowledge and conscious choices to live authentically. Just as the forest fire scorches the ground beneath the Sequoia cone, leaving it unharmed, yet coaxing it to open and release the seeds of its future . . . so do we experience our own fires that burn hot and threaten to destroy us. Yet, we cannot be destroyed. Spirit is eternal. And those fires, accepted as sparks of transformation, can release within us greater truth and clearer vision for the life we came to live.

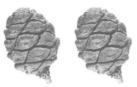

Act Two:
The Fires Come
-sharpening your spiritual skills

8 The Three-Headed Monster

"You gain strength, courage, and confidence by every experience in which you really stop to look fear in the face. You must do the thing which you think you cannot do."
– Eleanor Roosevelt

Author's Note: Discover how fear, doubt, and confusion are actually some of your best friends.

It is not easy to strike out on a path that diverges from the well-worn highways of the uninspired, ease seeking multitudes. Turning away from the beaten path and stepping into new territory is rarely encouraged. Oh, sure, you will hear dream inspired discussions espousing the bliss of living a purposeful life. But, actually walking to the beat of a different drum is often looked upon with skepticism and contempt. These are very mixed messages. When we understand the personal stake others have in keeping us *normal* and predictable, then we will begin to see the self-serving motivations of their concern for our *safety*.

I do not mean to make this all sound so sinister. Truthfully, most people who warn us of being unrealistic and starry-eyed in our life visions are doing what they think they must to protect us from the disappointment that they themselves have experienced. They really do believe they are looking out for our best interests and are doing us a favor to reel our lofty expectations back to earth.

But, unconsciously, while they strive to protect us, they are also heeding the commands of three powerful forces to which they have painfully acquiesced. We can see it in their eyes—submission. However reluctantly, they have already put away the dreams they had for their own lives, like how a child leaves behind a favorite toy when s/he begins the task of growing up. They admonish, "There are dreams . . . and then there is real life." And though our hearts lovingly shelter the dream's faint ember, we grow up as told, and fall into step with all the others who pretend it was all just a childish fantasy.

How did so many give up on their dreams? What smothered the blaze of passion born in each of them? Three imposters are most likely to blame—three illusions—three insidious thieves that steal confidence, hope, and inspiration. No strangers to any of us, we wrestle with them almost daily: fear, doubt, and confusion.

We battle valiantly with these fiends; hope against fear, confidence against doubt, and insight against confusion. Sometimes we win, but the victory is rarely permanent. We will contend with them throughout our lives as we step into new adventures.

Rather than fight these powers, if we understood their potential contributions to our lives, we could put away the battle and be open to the value they bring. Feelings of confusion, doubt, and fear are just moments in the transition from what was, to what is. That in-between place where the old way is fading and the new has yet to materialize. It can feel like you are losing everything that is familiar and predictable, but you are actually opening up to a higher level of life.

Fear is merely your survival instincts warning you of a *perceived* threat. Fear is the product of your limbic brain that provokes the fight or flight response. These mindless emotions are not thinking, logical reactions. They are purely instinctual and do not distinguish between degrees of threat. To your limbic brain, danger is simply danger. And the gut response is to run. But, you cannot run away from yourself, and the fear doesn't live anywhere but in your mind.

The interesting thing about fear is that *it* is what we are truly afraid of. It scares us to death. Once established, the fear itself becomes the focus of our attention. Fear feeds on itself and paradoxically grows stronger in the process. When U.S. President Franklin D. Roosevelt said, "The only thing we have to fear is fear itself; nameless, unreasoning, unjustified terror which paralyzes . . ." he could speak no truer words.

So how do you get the upper hand with this often unreasonable reaction? The way to stop fear is to befriend it. Befriend it? Yes. Step away from the emotion for a moment and just take a closer look at what your mind is telling you. Listen to its warnings of catastrophe and ruin. It is such a drama queen. Is what it is proposing logical? Is the disaster it is shrieking about likely to happen? Probably not.

Disconnect from the melodrama and try to hear the source of your fear's cry. It is trying to get your attention. It is concerned that you might be in harm's way. It is warning you, so that you may make a conscious choice. Listen and thank it. Reassure it that you are safe and that all is fine. Let trust hold fear's hand and fear will relax.

One of my biggest battles with fear happened many years ago when I took a dramatic change in my direction. I was living in Cleveland, Ohio, at the time. A company I had worked for relocated me there from Seattle, Washington, and then abruptly declared bankruptcy three months later! Now what? My then husband and I decided we were not crazy enough about Cleveland to stay, so we planned a move to San Francisco, California.

One morning, while he was at work and I sat idly watching a talk-variety show called *Alive and Well*, it struck me. I could do what *they* were doing! They were being the hosts of the show. They traveled the globe visiting fabulous vacation spots, played cook in the kitchen with master chefs making tantalizing desserts, and interviewed extraordinarily ordinary people who had found their calling in some hobby turned career. The three hosts had a ball. And why wouldn't they? They had a dream job. And it was easy! I could do that and (I smugly thought) I could probably do it better.

When my husband and I arrived in San Francisco, I determined that I would break into TV. What did it matter that San Francisco was the number five market in the nation and seasoned personalities in all the other ninety-five markets were vying like crazy to get in. I was bright, I was confident, I was sure the powers that be would see my potential and fall over backwards offering me lengthy, lucrative contracts. Did I mention that I was a bit naive?

One at a time, each flabbergasted TV station receptionist I called laughed her head off when I asked how I could get a job as a talk show host. They did offer me some useful advice though. Something about going to Podunk, Idaho, and paying my dues like everyone else.

My heart sank with each call, until I called an independent station and got a temp on the line. She actually talked to me. She told me the temp agency she worked for placed all the local broadcast jobs and I should call them. It was a long shot, but about then I was willing to follow *any* lead.

Sure enough, the temp agency placed me at the CBS television affiliate as a two week vacation replacement for the secretary in the news department. After a previous career selling tax sheltered investments to very well-to-do business owners, my new duties of sorting mail, answering phones, and typing (yes, we still typed back then) letters of apology to wannabe broadcasters (such irony!) was easy. They were so thrilled with my reliability that I was passed back and forth between news and engineering to cover the duties of several more vacationing employees.

I got up the courage one day to tell the news manager what I really wanted to do: host my own show. He had enough restraint to not laugh out loud, but instead told me that in the broadcast industry, videotape was your resume. I needed to have a tape to get anywhere. It must have been a slow news week because he gave me one-hour use of the news set, a teleprompter, and one cameraman to record a tape of me pretending to be a news anchor.

I prepared for four days. I selected real news stories, wrote the script and rehearsed for hours in my bathroom mirror. All my gumption and bravado dissolved slowing into the sweat running down my brow. My tongue had trouble navigating my mouth and my mind was so distracted that I couldn't keep my place in the script. And this was just in front of my home mirror. Doubt and panic were rapidly gaining ground. My blustery confidence blew itself out.

What if I froze on camera? What if lost my place? What if I stammered? What if I was so colossally horrible that the infamous grapevine announced my failure all over town and my chance for success ended before it began? What if they even fired me from the temp job? What if my name was mud for any other job in town? What if I could not earn enough money to pay my rent? What if I ended up on the streets? I could die!

Do you see what fear does when unmanaged? It takes a fleeting thought of concern and magnifies it into inescapable doom--all in a matter of a few seconds! The truth was I was not going to die. I knew that intellectually, but intellect does not govern emotions and never neutralizes fear. My fear was only saying, "Hey, you had better get a grip and nail this because you may never get another chance."

Once I heard fear's *real* message and focused on my goal, it stopped terrorizing me. The day of the shoot, I read my stories with confidence and believability, and my tyrannical mind was silent.

So, did the dream happen? Well, I didn't end up with my own talk show, but I did get a shot at being a field reporter in the San Francisco area for a while. Disproving the admonishment that I had to start in Podunk! Funny how keeping our eyes on the goal banishes fear.

Doubt, ironically, helps us learn to believe in ourselves. It challenges us to look at all we are capable of and to ask the really hard question: "Do I have what it takes?" Yes, you do! We all do. Each and every one of us has capabilities light-years beyond our wildest dreams.

People demonstrate this best when they face a crisis. Look at how strong people are. Look at how much ingenuity they have when faced with the unknown. The wealth of our personal power is lying dormant most of the time because we simply do not demand its presence. Life can get pretty ordinary when our extraordinary abilities are not given room to play.

Don't be afraid of your doubt. Just like fear, it is there to protect you. But, when you listen to the voice of doubt, do so with caution. Listen carefully to the feeble tales it weaves. Fear seems to be focused *externally*, but doubt is all about personal insecurity. It perpetually asks whether you are up to the challenge. It chinks away at self-confidence and plants seeds of uncertainty. Left unmanaged, doubt will paralyze you into a state of indecision.

Doubt is just your mind's way of asking the question, "Are you sure you can do this?" Remember all that you have done in the past? Look how far you have come. You have handled horrific events and grown stronger from the challenge. Never question your eternal power. You are far stronger than any situation you will ever face.

Oddly enough, confusion is the fertile ground of possibility—a dissonance in the routine that opens a door to new realities. When your mind is presented with something new, it can become very nervous because it has no past experience to draw upon in dealing with the new situation. The mind deals with current events based upon past experiences. But, if there is no relevant past experience, it does not know what to do. So, it will convince you that doing nothing is the safest choice. It will pretend it is confused, and that, until it is clear, you had best not make any decisions. Confusion is the mind's way of procrastinating. And yet it detests being confused, since the mind's purpose in life is to figure things out.

If left in confusion long, the mind will lure your attention back to what it *does* know . . . the past. It will remind you of all the wonderful things about the past and conveniently downplay all that was not so wonderful. It will lure you to retreat to what you already know. Even if it is not what you want, it will remind you of all that you will lose if you make a break from the past.

Do not be fooled into peeking over your shoulder at what you believe you are losing. You are losing nothing but the illusion of safety and comfort. And be honest . . . you weren't that comfortable anyway!

Picture confusion as a bridge connecting your been there, done that past, to your sky's the limit potential. Like fear, confusion's only power over you is keeping you from waking up and walking on. Confusion leads to more confusion—it is the snake eating its tail. Stay in confusion very long and fear and doubt will stealthily take up residence.

The only way out of this sinkhole is to take action. You must choose to not be mesmerized by the siren's song of this deadly trio. Fear, doubt, and confusion are only the unruly children of an unmanaged mind. They are self-created and have virtually nothing to do with your circumstances. Each can devastate you or act as your early warning system to become more aware. You must decide on a course of action and take it.

In your weakest state you are stronger than the best they will ever throw at you. You only need to be alert to their presence and watchful for a loss in your momentum. Resolve to move forward, even if only in baby steps. Choice, decision, and action are the antidotes to fear, doubt and confusion and will always defeat them. Any action, no matter how small, will disarm their spell. Successfully defeating these foes does not depend on the size of your step—it is found in your power to decide.

Keep your eyes trained only on the light of your dream. Feel it, taste it. When doubt, confusion or fear come creeping 'round, get moving! Take a small step toward your light. But, do it resolutely and quickly and they will vanish.

In our next chapter, we'll talk about a secret weapon that achievers use against the pull of inertia that fear, doubt and confusion can exert. If you've tried and failed, time and again, to make a change in your life, this chapter will change your fate and let you make steady progress toward your goal, even if it's enormous!

9 One Day at a Time

"How we spend our days is, of course, how we spend our lives."
– Annie Dillard

Author's Note: Are you relying on discipline to make change happen?
Discover the power of your subconscious and see lasting results.

One Day at a Time—you may recognize this oath of resolve from the Alcoholics Anonymous Twelve Step Program. Five simple words that shrink the enormity of personal change to one simple truth—today is the only day you need to deal with—a truth in every aspect of life. Especially when it comes to change, large or small, what you do *today* will ensure or defeat change.

How many times have you failed to make real change happen in your life? It is tough enough admitting to the need for change, but nothing happens until you make a decision and do not turn back. And that is where many of us inevitably give up. We make fervent resolutions to stop smoking, lose weight, improve our relationships, and save money. We are serious! *This* time we will do it. And, in the first week or so, we are champions of self-discipline. But, time passes, old habits lure us back, and our good intentions dissolve bit by bit. Who among us does not know the weight of that defeat? It is humbling to realize that a habit can be stronger than our will.

But, not everyone succumbs to the pull of inertia. Some people actually set their sights on a desire and progressively make the necessary changes to reach their goal. Are they special, or maybe blessed in some way that we are not? Do they know something we have not really considered? Let's talk about two powerful things they do to make sure changes stick.

First, they do not see the change as an enormous feat, even if it seems so. They keep their end result in mind, but focus their actions on what they need to do *today*. Most of us have a built-in aversion to difficulty and drudgery. We know we can do even the most grueling things for a short while. But, if reaching our goal requires that we keep constant vigilance for a long time, we practically feel defeated before we even begin.

Let's say that you truly want to stop smoking. If I asked you to not smoke just for today, could you do it? A single day would not seem an eternity and most smokers would say they could quit smoking . . . just for today. But, when faced with the prospect of never smoking ever again, the burden can seem overwhelming. The will to not smoke for even one day is overpowered by imagining the challenge of the endless days to come.

But, the simple truth is, today is the *only* day that you need to have discipline. Don't worry about all the tomorrows ahead of you. Each one of them is just one day, like today is just one day to stay the course; just one day to do what you say you will do. Before you know it, you will have made it through a day without a passing thought to smoking. Habits *do* break—if we give them a chance.

Those who consistently achieve their goals also know that life seeks equilibrium. It likes consistency and it makes whatever changes it needs to maintain the status quo. Life behaves like a room temperature thermostat. If that thermostat is set to 72°F and the room temperature drops below that, it will turn the heater on to bring the room back to the preset temperature. If the temperature rises above 72°F, it will turn the heater off until the proper setting is achieved.

In scientific circles this phenomenon of equilibrium is known as a balancing system. A balancing system's purpose is to maintain a specific predetermined condition. Any deviation from the desired situation will trigger a countering action to bring it back to stability.

How can you use the power of equilibrium to your advantage? Perhaps you would like to lose the fifteen pounds that have slowly crept up on you in the past five years. At this moment in time, your *thermostat* is set to maintain your current body weight. As much as you might like to lose those excess pounds, there are forces exerting pressure to keep the weight on. Until you know what those forces are, and the influence they exert, your efforts to slim down will be temporary at best.

This is the biggest reason so many people experience a yo-yo effect while dieting. They change eating habits and lifestyle behaviors long enough to reach their goal, then go right back to old habits that put the weight on in the first place. They never got to the core of change—modifying behaviors permanently. They only changed long enough to see a result and then reverted back to habits that destroyed all their progress.

To keep the weight off, you need to know what caused the weight gain over the years. Did your eating habits change? Did your lifestyle become more sedentary? Did you have an injury that physically slowed you down and let the pounds pile up? Did you enter a new stage of life where your body chemistry shifted? Did your life become more stressful? Under stress bodies tend to layer on the padding, or protection. Whatever the reason, your body began to accommodate the circumstances and then it reset the thermostat to maintain the new weight.

To change any situation, you need to change the elements that created that situation. Find out what contributed to the situation you would like to change, and then begin to change the contributing factors. Situations are the outcome of specific actions. Change the actions and you will change the situation.

Nadia looked at her world and saw a need that she knew she could uniquely fill. But all did not go smoothly. So she diligently kept trying new avenues to make this dream happen. She didn't give up, because she believed in the rightness of her dream and was patient enough to find the right combination for success.

"I live in Scotland and I'm so saddened by the number of homeless we have. No one should have to live on the streets. It's a rich country. So, three years ago I decided to help.

I'm Italian and food is very important to Italians. It's the whole social thing and everything revolves around food. If you go to a wedding and the foods not right, it's not a success. If you're happy, you eat. If you're sad, you eat. All good things happen at the dinner table.

For me, having food and a roof over your head are basic necessities. So, my idea was born from matching my love of cooking with the need of the homeless. I decided to publish an Italian cookbook and use the proceeds to donate to the homeless. Plus, I wanted to show people that Italian cooking isn't that hard and it's healthy. My family and I have created these recipes over a period of sixty years.

For over three years, I have written to so many publishers, celebrity chefs, radio stations, and homeless charities to see if they would publish the book. I do not want the credit for the recipe book and only want to help the homeless people. Unfortunately, I have had so many refusals and no offers—in three years!

Your message has helped me to keep pursuing my dream to have the recipe book published. I am sure there will be someone out there who will think this is a great idea. I try to keep my dream alive by talking to people about it and giving them samples of the book.

I have a busy life being a wife, mother of two girls, and working a part-time job. I can't always give my dream all the attention I would like to. However, I do keep chipping away at it by either writing a letter, making a telephone call, etc. Like you said, *one day at a time.*

One great thing, which has happened in the last couple of months, is that samples of my recipe book will be sold to help raise funds for the school, which my girls attend. They are really enthusiastic about it, and the pupils will even do some artwork for it.

I was also asked to attend one of the cookery sessions as ten fourteen year old girls were trying out five of the recipes. They did a brilliant job, and they presented them so well, too. The great thing was that they were so amazed that they could produce such good dishes. I am hoping that this may help young people look at eating healthier diets and to see how easy the recipes are!

My point is that you have to keep working at your dream and

sometimes it may go off in different directions, and you may need to adjust. But, keep going with your dream. There are times I get down about my progress, but I know that something good will come. As long as I can keep going and not let it die, something will happen.

You challenged me to not quit and to look beyond the normal way of doing things. This is important to me, but it's not been easy. But, I'm not giving up. I'll keep chipping away at it and doing whatever I can, and I know that eventually I'll succeed, because it's just too right not to.

Still no offers of publishing my recipe book. However, the school, where my children attend, has sold over 500 copies and are still selling copies of my cookbook! I have been doing more cooking demos with the pupils, which I love doing. To raise funds, I cooked for a dinner party for eight people. That dinner party raised £1,200.

I am also doing cooking demos with homeless people on a monthly basis using the recipes from my book. The sessions are going really well and after they have cooked the dishes we all sit down and eat it. I have been told that they really are getting a lot from cooking and sharing the food. What's great for me is to see the recipes working and they're so pleased with themselves with their cooking creations.

I am confident that something will happen with my recipe book. It is just a question of when. It's a big world out there and I am sure someone, somewhere will want to publish it!" –Nadia Alonzi

Nadia keeps her eye on her dream, but does what she needs to do today to make it happen.

So, let's examine a change you would like to achieve. Draw a vertical line down the center of a sheet of paper dividing it in half. At the top of the left column write: Reasons to Change. At the top of the right column write: What's Keeping Me Stuck.

On the left side of the paper list all the reasons why you want to change. Include personal desires as well as any external pressures. In our smoking example, you might want to stop smelling like smoke and yellowing your teeth and fingernails. Maybe your family is urging you to stop for your health, as well as theirs. Perhaps your doctor has warned you that a suspicious spot on your lung x-ray might be the beginning of a cancer. Maybe your health insurance company is levying premium hikes due to your high-risk habit. You could look at what you spend on cigarettes over the course of a year and imagine spending that on a vacation, instead. You might recognize that you are setting an example for your children that you do not want them to follow. Maybe you are just tired of being banned to the outdoors to maintain your habit—especially in the winter. Or you are scared by your lack of breath in climbing only one flight of stairs. These scenarios are all strong forces *to* change.

If you have tried to make a change and failed, there are probably unconsidered and unattended countering forces at play in your life. To consider these forces, on the right side of the paper list all the factors conspiring to keep things the way they currently are. What is perpetuating the situation? With our smoking example, divorcing yourself from the identity of *being* a smoker can be hard. It has become part of who you are, or at least part of what you do. There is also a physical, as well as psychological, addiction to overcome. Some of your social friendships might be based in smoking. For instance, are all of the people you take breaks with at work smokers? If you stop smoking will those friendships fade? I once heard a manager say that he would like to stop smoking, but he felt his access to company insider information would suffer if he didn't attend the regular smoking breaks that his peers took. Maybe your spouse smokes, making it hard to escape the constant temptation. Perhaps you are currently disease-free and you feel no urgency to quit.

Whatever your current situation, there are forces fighting any change you try to initiate. Your goal has to be stronger than the status quo or it will not survive. And the first step is to disempower current habits by recognizing how you are contributing to the way things are now.

Motivational speaker Tony Robbins says that everything we do is aimed at either experiencing pleasure or avoiding pain. The exercise above will help you determine the pleasure you are experiencing from *not* changing and the pain you imagine you *will* experience in changing. These are the factors that keep you stuck. He also says that, of the two, the avoidance of pain is stronger than the desire for pleasure. It is a survival instinct to avoid pain. So, if the change you want appears to be fraught with more pain than pleasure and the status quo appears to provide more pleasure than pain, your natural instinct will be to subconsciously fight the change so you can avoid pain. Being aware of this tendency, you can take control and use the forces of pleasure and pain to your advantage.

There are four variables you can affect to swing the momentum in favor of your desired change.

1. Increase the pain of today's situation to make your current reality more intolerable.
2. Decrease the pleasure of today's situation to make your current reality less desirable.
3. Increase the pleasure of tomorrow's goal to make your goal more enticing and compelling.
4. Decrease the perceived pain of reaching tomorrow's goal to make it less formidable.

Here are some ideas that can help.

If you wish to stop smoking:

- Switch to a brand of cigarette whose taste you don't like.
- Watch yourself in the mirror as you smoke.
- Get your family and friends to consistently remind you of your desire to quit.
- For every cigarette you smoke throw one away (increases the pain of paying for your habit).
- Do not empty the ashtray to see and smell how ripe it can get.
- Walk down a park trail and pick up cigarette butts left by other smokers.
- Tell your family and friends you will pay them ten dollars every time they see you smoke or smell smoke on you.
- Talk to a hospital patient who is dying of lung cancer caused by smoking.
- Drive by a hangout for young people and watch as children smoke—imagine that they are *your* children—and then remember the patient with cancer.
- Ask your doctor to show you pictures of cancerous lungs, and throat and mouth ulcers caused by smoking.
- Buy your cigarettes one pack at a time. Make easy access to cigarettes difficult.
- Give your cigarettes to a spouse or coworker so you have to ask them each time you want to smoke. Remember, it will cost you ten dollars when you do!
- Switch to unfiltered cigarettes so you get the full, undiluted *taste*.
- Imagine the vacation you could take each year with the money you could save by not smoking.

If you want to lose weight:

- Make yourself eat that favorite snack while watching yourself in a mirror.
- Instead of having only one slice of pie, force yourself to eat it until you are close to gagging.
- Stand naked in front of the mirror when you have your favorite naughty snack.
- Put on your skinny clothes for a few hours a day and feel how uncomfortable you are.
- Hold your nose while eating (it reduces the sensation of taste).
- Put a picture of an extremely obese person on your snack cupboard or refrigerator.
- Put all favorite snacks in a locked box in a difficult to get to area of your home. Better yet, take them to a neighbor to keep so you have to go ask to have your fix.
- Let someone else do the grocery shopping and don't allow them

to buy off limits snacks.
- Talk with someone who has made the changes you want to make. Find out just how hard it really was. Most will say that *deciding* to change was much harder than making the change.
- Ask yourself, which is worse, the inconvenience of breaking a habit or living the rest of your shortened life with poor health.
- Imagine the pleasure of being alive when your great-grandchildren are born!
- Think of all the experiences you will have in the rest of your life because you stayed healthy.
- Envision your friends green with envy when they are all wearing plus-sized clothes and you are still slim and agile.
- Imagine knowing at the end of your life that you lived a long, full, enriching, and healthy life.
- Buy snacks, if you must, in the trial or snack size only, not two pound bags of chips!

I know you can come up with many, many more. And it is best that you do. The techniques you relate to most will be most effective. The real trick is consistency, so put a plan in place that *makes* you stay on track. Changing habits is the first step to realizing the new reality you are after. And changing habits is best done with the knowledge and assistance of others. It is too easy to let yourself off the hook. Being accountable to a family member or friend is more difficult, but also more effective in achieving the goal you are after.

Remember, change happens one day at a time. Today is the *only* day that you need to walk the path toward your new reality. Just today. If you slip, get back up . . . right now—not tomorrow, not next week. The moment you give into the past, admit it and remember what you are trying to achieve.

"Every day I say to myself that today is tomorrow! Every choice I make today is going to effect tomorrow. So, if I make the choice to eat good and work out and stay positive, I have more energy and then I can deal with everything else better. If I decide to eat this one thing, in the long run that might not seem like a big thing. But, now I think, if I eat that, how am I going to feel afterwards? I'm more conscious in trying to make better choices so I will feel better. I can do this!"
—Sheila O'Cooney

Look back at your own list of current pain and future pleasure. There is nothing on earth that is stronger than your conscious will. You must simply decide and decide decisively! What quality of life do you want? Ask that question whenever you are facing old habits and you will defeat the old status quo and create new habits that will support your chosen life.

But, when you make the decision—MAKE IT. Don't vacillate and go back on your word. Don't decide one way today and change your mind tomorrow. If you find yourself unable to make or even keep a promise to yourself, maybe it's time to stop making choices with your mercurial mind and to rely upon a deeper level of resolve: one born of an eternal clarity. In the next chapter, Decidophobia, we'll look beyond decisions made with the mind and see how to tap into a stronger and eternal reservoir of knowing.

# 10   Decidophobia

"The intellect has little to do on the road to discovery. There comes a leap in consciousness, call it intuition or what you will, and the solution comes to you and you don't know how or why."
–Albert Einstein

Author's Note: Should you? Shouldn't you? Overcome indecision and learn a new way of making life-enriching decisions.

You have been putting it off for far too long. You know that. But, the thought of making a mistake keeps you paralyzed. Like a deer frozen in the headlights of an oncoming car, you wait in agony for the inevitable to happen and hope you can deal with it.

Decidophobia: the fear of decisions. We have all been there. Knowing that we have to make up our minds and make a move, but not at all confident about what that move should be. Stuck between one direction and the other. Trying to imagine what life would be like after THE DECISION. Either choice you make has its duality of good and bad possibilities. Neither is a clear winner. So, you put it off hoping the sky will open, lightning will strike, and the voice of God will boom forth the answer. But you hear nothing.

So, how do you get out of this limbo? Flip a coin? List the pros and cons? Let someone else finally get sick of waiting and decide for you? Or do you decide not to decide . . . which is still a decision. Or you consider, "Maybe, if the decision is so unclear, just maybe staying where I am is safer. It feels safer anyway."

And there it is—defeat and mediocrity. You and your life are going with the flow; not making waves; not rocking the boat; being in the moment; and trusting the universe—whatever! No matter how you dress it up, you simply chickened out and you know it.

The funny thing is, you already know what you should do. You always have. But, you want a guarantee that you are going to live happily ever after. Since you cannot foretell the future, your mind jumps in and pushes all the fear buttons; it knows you after all these years. So, you and your mind set about what-if-ing until you hang your head in defeat and settle for mediocrity.

All this turmoil created by you because you are missing one fundamental truth. *Knowing* is not a function of the mind. Of course, your mind will instantly reject this thought. It *has* to. Its survival is dependent upon convincing you that it is the center of all you know. Like the bully in the schoolyard, it cannot afford for you to think it is not the supreme authority in your life.

But the simple truth is, it is not. The mind is a very specific tool that we've been erroneously taught to use for everything. It is very good at coming up with options. It can dream up all kinds of possibilities and imagine every single outcome. It can weigh the consequences of a decision and choose the most logical path. But it cannot, and does not, guarantee that it is right. No matter what it tells you, it does not *know*. Knowing resides much deeper in your being. Knowing is about truth, not options. Truth is constant. Options are circumstantial. Truth is not intellectual. You do not *think* it up. Truth was there before you were born and will be there after you are gone. It is eternal.

How do you access this place of knowing? Try this. Close your eyes and think of a dilemma that you are facing right now. For a moment, just listen to the chatter in your mind surrounding this situation. Notice how confused and conflicting your thoughts are. Watch how your mind runs and reruns scenarios of failure and disaster. A confused mind can only generate fear. It goes nuts when it cannot figure it out. Do not get caught up in its self fabricated anxiety. These are just emotional reflexes to your mind's confusion; they are not prophetic. Just pretend that you are eavesdropping on someone else's thoughts. Create distance between you and your emotions so that you can find your balance again.

When you can observe your emotions with a bit of detachment, they can be quite entertaining. The drama. The suspense. You are *not* your thoughts or your emotions, and they are not necessarily the truth. They just happen.

Thoughts of fear and anxiety originate in your limbic brain. You have several regions of your brain that serve very different purposes. Your cerebral cortex is your logical brain. It reasons and problem solves. Your limbic brain is your most primitive brain. It is the fight or flight control center. It is not logical and does not really *think*. It merely reacts; and usually out of fear. No wonder all the feelings it generates are of doom and gloom!

When you have truly reached a state of being, as the observer of your thoughts, when you are no longer alarmed by them or even believe them, then turn the volume down on your mind's chatter. Imagine all that noise behind a door that is slowly closing until you can only hear a faint hum. Sit silently, inside and out, and listen to the quiet. Do not think. Remember, the answer is not in thought.

I find that if I hold my hand over my heart and imagine breathing with my heart, it helps me stay out of my head and not get caught up in the thoughts. This tends to quiet my mind and focuses my attention at a deeper level. I then ask, "What is my truth?" I listen, not for a thought, but for a feeling. I keep asking the question until I feel a settling in my heart, a grounded-ness. I feel an "of course." This is how *my* knowing feels. Yours may feel different. But, it will feel right and familiar to you. Truth always does.

Try this with a perplexing decision you have been putting off. See if you can find a direct path to your own knowing. Do not question that it is there. It is. Your reasoning brain has no place in this activity. If it knew what you should do, it would have told you by now. Instead, develop the skill of listening to your inner wisdom. It requires stillness and quiet. It is always talking to you, but the noise of life can drown it out.

For every problem you face, there is an answer. It is not always easy to hear. It does not always make logical sense. But, the answer is always present when the question arises. By developing this new skill you will end the agony of your confused mind. Confusion is agonizing . . . knowing is clear. Clarity has no what ifs. It does not second-guess. There is no chatter. Clarity will not come in the form of a thought. It will present itself as a feeling. Trust your feelings. They will tell you the truth. Thoughts often lie, but feelings never do.

In our next chapter, Surrender, we'll take the act of deciding to the next level. For even after we make a decision, we can experience defeat. Sometimes we need to learn to get out of our own way and stop pushing so hard.

11 Surrender?

"Some of us think holding on makes us strong;
but sometimes it is letting go."
–Unknown

Author's Note: Chasing happiness? Find out how your approach
may be defeating you.

For most of my life I have valued one thing above all else: independence. Maybe the craving for independence is built into the American genetic code or maybe it was the byproduct of being the oldest child or regaining my footing after two failed marriages. I could conjure up many reasons, but in the long run, reasons don't matter. Independence was my god, and I worshipped control. As it turned out, my obsession with independence provided the fertile ground for the seedlings of my biggest life lesson—to let go.

From as long ago as I can remember, I have been haunted by those words. *Let Go.* They hid in the shadow of my every action. When I argued for my cause, I heard their faint whisper. When I struggled to make sense of heartaches, their seductive music echoed softly just inside my ear . . . *let go* . . .

The words literally terrified me. To me, letting go meant giving up, conceding, and relinquishing control. Letting go of control meant losing my independence. It meant surrendering. To surrender seems so wrong! It contradicted every survival instinct I had. Even its definition was unpalatable: to yield, to give up to the power of another.

Never!

Yet, *Let Go* did not let go of me. Slowly I began to understand this tenacious stalker. Like many truths, the lesson was buried in the experience of its opposite. I learned the worth of letting go by stubbornly hanging on.

After years of struggle, I began to notice that the tighter my grip on control, the less I *felt* in control. Whenever I adamantly defended my independence, I felt most *dependent*. Whenever I pushed to get what I wanted most, my zealous attempts to achieve it were thwarted.

I believed so much in the rightness of my force-and-control strategy that when my efforts inevitably failed, I believed that I just hadn't tried hard enough. I figured that if I just pushed harder I would surely get the prize, or so it seemed.

Little by little, I became blinded to any other way of seeing. For me, success could only be achieved by ultimate drive and absolute control. Even if I was not experiencing success, I believed that it was just a matter of time and will. All the success gurus reinforced that approach.

My efforts seemed to get in the way as much as they promised fulfillment. It began to dawn upon me that I was missing a piece of the puzzle. Try hard wasn't working.

I remember waking up to the reality that trying hard might not be the answer when I was working with a team of trainers with a previous employer. I had found what I believed was the most exciting new process for training that I'd ever seen. Before introducing it to my peers, I studied it and read everything I could get my hands on about it. It was truly ingenious. I excitedly told them about it at one of our staff meetings. I explained how this process would revolutionize our systems and approaches to training and how it would yield much better results than we were getting. I went on and on, my passion about the discovery bubbling over into the greatest sales job of all time!

Imagine my shock when they were unmoved. They said they liked the idea, but no one got on board that train of passion with me. I walked away feeling confused and disappointed. I'm a very passionate person and I've always consciously used that energetic influence to ignite the passion in others. It had worked without fail, until now.

It wasn't until a few weeks later that a friend, present at that meeting, explained why I had failed to rally the troops. Her words seared through me. "Your excitement for this idea was so strong and so encompassing that you didn't leave any room for *our* participation. You never once asked us what we thought. You just kept plowing and assumed that we were all on board. There was no room for us in *your* vision."

The harder I'd tried to influence them, the less influenced they were. Sometimes when we try hard, we become blind to our results and to alternatives to getting what we want. Without her insight and feedback, I would have never known why my efforts had failed.

Can we learn to see our own blindness? To open our eyes to a new reality? A reality that totally contradicts everything we believe to be true? Is it possible that the actions we take to achieve what we want are the very actions that defeat us? Read that last sentence again. Your mind won't want to accept that thought. It's not logical. But, remember, your perception of logic is dictated by what you believe to be true. What if what you believe to be true isn't true? I believed that extreme passion would move mountains. Instead, it dug a hole!

By waking up to a different way of seeing, we can sometimes break free of chains we didn't even know we wore. Billie found herself, years down the road of her life, asking a very different question about her future. A question that revealed a whole new world to her.

"A little more than three years ago I saw that I had spent twenty-eight years working for someone else and franticly racing around with schedules, career, and raising kids. All the things we're told that will lead to success. But, I could see that it was a tread mill that I was never going to win no matter how hard I kept pushing, pushing, PUSHING.

I had spent about four years learning more about allowing spirit to guide my life and through meditation and trusting that the Supreme Being had better things planned for me. So, I quit my job, packed up a five bedroom house, and started what I call my *walk about*.

I'd always been a compulsive doer, a giant list maker, volunteer extraordinaire, lawn specialist, etc. It was probably the hardest decision I ever made, but here I was in my little truck all packed and ready to camp across the USA.

Washington to Florida—that was my goal. I didn't plan everyday out or when and where I was going to be. I simply surrendered to what spirit had in store for me.

Well, from the start I knew I was on the right track. My little truck that never got more than twenty-two miles to the gallon was now getting thirty. Yes, I doubled checked and that is what I was getting. I still am.

I no longer worry about what I am doing or where the money is going to come from. It just does. I am now cooking and cleaning houses in the wheat country. I have a rent free house for feeding a couple of horses and a donkey (he loves me). I have a great garden with a sprinkler system. And I no longer have to take tons of blood pressure medicine.

By surrendering all my concerns and worries to spirit I am better taken care of than I ever was able to take care of my self, and my life is so much fuller."—Billie S.

Billie took a big chance and walked away, not only from a way of life, but from a way of being. She learned that surrendering the control she *thought* was keeping her world together, actually made room for the natural flow of her life to enter.

It's hard to imagine that something we believe to be so right can be so wrong. Can giving up control really allow things to function more smoothly and naturally? What if holding on leaves us empty-handed? What if wielding power makes us impotent? What if surrendering isn't losing, but receiving what we most want? What if ultimate strength isn't rigidity, but willingness? What if we have it all backwards?

I have found this to be true for me. The more I pursued happiness, the faster it ran from me. The more I wanted success, the less likely it became. I fought with every fiber of my being for what I wanted . . . and found myself empty-handed.

Buddhism professes that all pain comes from struggle and resistance. I had believed that struggle was *required* to achieve what I wanted. However, *my* plan wasn't working. So I began to ask a different question. I stopped asking, "How can I *make* this work?" and began to ask, "How *does* this work?"

Consider a river as it flows along its banks. It does not complain about the boulders lying midstream, it simply flows around them. It does not resist gravity's pull down the mountainside; it simply cooperates with the natural law guiding its progress. It surrenders; it lets go. Because it cooperates with the nature of the system in which it lives, it is one of the most powerful forces on earth.

When we feel compelled to control things, it's usually not because we know how things should be. It's often because we are afraid that we will get lost in the chaos of the unknown. So, we define the path and strictly adhere to that definition. We become rigid and unable to access the ideas and resources that the path naturally attracts. We close off all other contributions, fearing it will loosen our grip. Little do we realize that it is our grip that is strangling our chance for success. When we let go, we are able to access the abundant resources that show up to play.

Where have you been needlessly struggling? What are you failing to control? Where are you reaping the exact opposite of what you truly want? Are you open to a different possibility?

Imagine hacking your way through the jungle with a machete in full swing only to cut through to a cleared path already leading to your destination. Imagine for a moment that your struggle is totally self created—totally unnecessary. Stop struggling long enough to look around and see if there is a cleared path in front of you.

If the choices you've been making are not getting you what you want, then perhaps it's time to try something radically different! Beware that your mind will tell you it's not reasonable to get what you want. Know that it will feel uncomfortable to try something radically different. Others will question your about-face and many will believe you to be delusional. All new perceptions are met with such resistance. Certainly, in 1539, Copernicus felt the oppression of his peers who thought that his declaration that the earth revolved around the sun, not the sun around the earth, was blasphemy. They could not conceive of such a view because they were so convinced of their own rightness. In truth, they just could not see beyond their beliefs.

If you are truly looking for what works, then you need to think beyond your beliefs. You need to realize that there are many realities that exist outside of your awareness at any moment in time. It's a fine line between having a belief and being *had by* a belief. A new idea cannot penetrate a tightly closed mind. Surrendering to the possibility that there is a different way of living your life other than exerting severe control can open the doors to your own discovery.

In the next chapter we'll look at how our unconscious beliefs can do more than blind us to other possibilities. They can sabotage the very desires we're after. Driving with the Brake On may give you a new way to find traction on the path of your dream.

12 Driving with the Brake On

"Once we become aware of how much our daily experiences are influenced by our inner programs, the more imperative it becomes to examine our beliefs and be prepared to change those beliefs that are limiting us."
— John Kehoe

Author's Note: Is your life stalled and going in circles? Find out how to release the brakes and achieve what you really want.

In the winter of 1984 I rented a U-Haul truck to move cross-country from Cleveland, Ohio, to San Francisco, California. The incredibly long journey was made even longer by the truck's persistently sluggish speed. No matter how hard I stomped on the gas pedal, the truck would go no faster than forty-five miles per hour.

After miles of frustration, increasingly vile thoughts, and exhausted leg muscles, I pulled into the only town I had seen for hours. I was in Texas. After failing to get help at two gas stations, I learned a new lesson—people who work at gas stations do not repair cars anymore, not even in Texas.

I hoped against hope to find an open mechanic's shop. It was Sunday. Fortune finally smiled on me, and I came upon a tiny shop on the outskirts of town. I pulled in and a robust man with overalls as greasy and black as his filthy floor strolled over to ask how he could help. I told him of my dilemma and my hopes to arrive in California before growing old! He popped the truck's hood and smiled. "U-Haul sometimes installs speed governors on their trucks, and you got one of them."

"What is a speed governor?" I asked.

"It limits how fast you can go, as you found out. The accelerator will only depress enough to reach the speed U-Haul chooses. They figure that most folks moving their own furniture and stuff are not very experienced at driving trucks this size, so they make sure you don't go faster than you can handle," he concluded.

"Can you disengage it or whatever you have to do to make it go faster?" I pleaded.

"Nope. Against regulations," he said, a bit too smugly.

"*A mechanic with ethics,*" I glibly mumbled to myself. Well, at least I knew why all my efforts to gain speed were fruitless. All the while that I had been stomping on the gas, the truck was applying the brakes!

I once heard a financial consultant say that each of us will only make as much money as we believe we are worth. He warned that our financial futures were limited by a *money governor.* Just like that governor limited the speed of my trip, a money governor will limit how much financial momentum we achieve.

Each of us operates under a particular standard of personal wealth. That standard was set long ago by our parents' beliefs about money and the lifestyle we lived as a child. The financial status of the friends we had then, as well as the prevailing influences of our childhood community also helped forge that financial model. Each factor colluded to create a level of *normal* for us. And for us, normal is reality.

Intellectually we might *think* we deserve much more money than we have, but deep in our subconscious, we have exactly what we are comfortable having. On those occasions when we earn or have much more than our normal funds, we seem blindly compelled to get rid of it quickly. We either spend it—sometimes frivolously or sometimes unexpectedly—like an expense to replace your vehicle's transmission or to handle an increase in property taxes, or whatever pops up to siphon off the excess cash. It seems that when we exceed our money comfort zone, the world and we conspire to do whatever it takes to get back to normal.

I can imagine the groans of disbelief now. But, consider this for a moment. When was the last time you made or had money that *far* surpassed your usual finances? What happened to that excess? Did you use it to secure your future or put it to use making even more money through wise investments?

Did you splurge on something that in hindsight seemed rather foolish? Maybe you took the recommendation of a friend and bought shares of a highly speculative stock. Maybe you just squandered it away and ended up with little to show for it at all. Chances are, if you are like most of us, whatever you did with it, you soon found yourself right back at the same net worth that you had before the windfall.

Ponder this revealing statistic: eight out of ten lottery winners declare bankruptcy within five years of winning the jackpot? Eighty percent! And these are folks who won millions of dollars! The problem was, that instant wealth was being handled by a non-millionaire mind. A mind with non millionaire habits of managing money.

It is much like a typical college student in their freshman year of college. For many, this is the first taste of real independence from the parental restrictions they endured in the past. Suddenly, they can go where they want, when they want, for as long as they want. They can do what they want, whenever they want. And with little to no accountability to anyone in authority, many students spend a great part of their first college year engaging in behaviors that would shock their parents. Kids rebel and flaunt their newly found freedom . . . until one day they wake up to the inevitable reality that their irresponsibility has been personally damaging.

And so it is with many of the instant lottery millionaires created every day. With all that new money, they sometimes go a little crazy and buy incredibly expensive things just because, suddenly, they can. Mesmerized by burgeoning bank accounts, they proceed to spend their windfall like it will last forever. But, pretty soon—sooner than they ever dreamed—the money is gone, the bills are piled up, and their bank balance once again reflects their true money sophistication. It shrinks to their *normal* level of funds. Back to what is comfortable. And the promise of a life of ease disappears as quickly as the money did.

This notion of a governor started me wondering what other parts of our lives might be limited by unnoticed governing beliefs.

Perhaps we only have as much happiness as we believe we deserve. After all, if we walk around happy all the time, someone or something is sure to take it away. We do not want to invite scrutiny. And why do we merit such happiness when the world around us is filled with so much unhappiness? Maybe being that happy, especially for no logical reason, is just being naive. And God knows, with all the wrongs we have committed in our lives, we don't really deserve to be feeling so good.

Maybe we get only as much love as we believe we are due. Again, we're nothing special, just one person making it through life. With all our faults, and we know them well, why would anyone truly love us? So, we end up suspicious of those who care, knowing that we do not deserve it. We might not even let that love in, since we know it will likely end badly anyway. Many folks just decide to avoid the whole issue of love altogether thinking that there's too much vulnerability— too many chances to get hurt.

Do we have a worthiness governor that limits our level of confidence or self-worth to a paltry level that someone like us *ought* to have? After all, it's wise to know your place.

We could go on and on. In just about every aspect of our lives, we have developed a comfort with a certain quality of existence. Too much less than that level causes pain and too much more causes anxiety. So, we stay within our self defined boundaries of normality and make adjustments when we stray too far away.

Consequently, your life, for better or worse, is a diary of who you have believed you are. No point in disagreeing. If you truly believed you could be and have more, you would. There is no judgment in that. Not really. It is just factual. You have become the version of you that you have *chosen* to be. You have become the you that you are comfortable with, as one of my "Waking Up" readers woke up to.

"Why am I spinning my wheels? Why does this constantly happen to me? What is going on that I can't press forward? I read your message about the governor and I said, 'She's absolutely correct!' In the job I have right now, I'm taking on a lot of responsibilities and not getting the recognition for it. When I read your governor message, what that said to me was, '*I'm* doing it.' The reason that this is constantly happening to me is because my mental governor is saying I have to do a lot for everyone, to keep on taking on more and more and more. And don't expect, or don't even ask for the recognition. I need to move out of the governor thing where I'm going 45 miles an hour, and I'm pressing my foot to the accelerator. I need to . . . I want to go faster.

I have, this week, consciously been setting limits for myself where I'm saying no. To me, that is actually moving my governor, because I'd never say no before and I'm starting to do that. It's a little scary for me, but I'm actually getting a reaction to it where they're saying, 'Gee, we should have recognized you. Yes, you are doing the work of three people.' So, I'm liking that part."—Toni D.

Do you really want more money, more love, and more happiness? Then stop chasing after a new job, a new romance or greater thrills. The thrill of something new will lift your spirits for a moment or two. But, newness wears off and your life will once again look remarkably the same as it did before. Remember the governor. Without changing its limiting settings, getting more money, love or happiness will be temporary at best.

Your beliefs about who you really are are much stronger than the circumstances you find yourself in. Just changing your surroundings isn't enough to experience a new life. You need to change how you think of yourself and what you believe is possible.

Work on the governor, not the world. Find out why you have chosen to have what you have and not what you say you want. What is holding you back? What sabotaging beliefs limit your choices? Why don't you believe you deserve more?

The good news is that all of your limiting beliefs and your habitual comfort zones are merely safe choices you once made and kept making. They were just choices, like what to wear today.

But, for you, tomorrow can be a very different day from today. You can choose to let more love, more happiness, and more money in. You can choose to believe you are worth all of it—and even more. Or, instead, you can choose to believe that even if you *did*, by some fluke, get what you really wanted, it wouldn't last anyway, so why bother.

In this lifetime, on this planet, experience is all we have. What are you choosing to experience? Why? Figure that out and you will advance to a higher order of will—a stronger discipline to choose according to your values. You won't long for the healing of a strained relationship, yet continue to behave distant and angry. You won't wish for an end to your money worries, but continue to spend excessively. You will make conscious choices and stop unwittingly sabotaging your results.

There is so much of everything in this life. You are as deserving as the next soul. Being happy, being rich, having a rewarding life—these are not evil. You are not taking anything away from anyone else. Quite the contrary, in a state of abundance, you will be a wonderful gift of an example to the world. One that will hopefully inspire others to break free from their self-limiting governors too, and contribute greatness to the world, governed by conscious will, not mindless comfort.

But, to reach that state of abundance, first we need to do some work on our thoughts and how we direct our will. In the next chapter, we'll dig deep into the mire of the belief in lack and see that abundance truly is our natural state . . . if we just stop preventing it.

13 Out of the Land of Lack

"The world is full of abundance and opportunity, but far too many people come to the fountain of life with a sieve instead of a tank car . . . a teaspoon instead of a steam shovel. They expect little and as a result they get little."
—Ben Sweetland

Author's Note: Are you good at manifesting lack? Rejoice! Learn how to create abundance with just a slight change in aim.

Is a law absolute? Does it always apply? Is the effect of that law consistent? It depends greatly upon the law you consider. Man-made laws seem controlled by the dictates of the society in which the laws exist. For instance, the punishment for someone convicted of killing another human being depends on the soundness of the evidence, on the sympathies of the jury, on the impartiality of the judge, and on the political ties of the defendant. It also depends on which county, state, or even country in which the defendant is prosecuted. The penalty is not absolute . . . it is very conditional.

Then there are natural laws—laws of the physical sciences—that supersede the whims of man. Two of these laws are *Newton's Law of Gravity* and *Newton's First Law of Motion*, which state that a body continues in its state of constant velocity (which may be zero) unless it is acted upon by an external force. These laws have consistent and predictable results. It does not matter if you believe in them or even like them. They still work the same. If you let go of your keys, they will drop. If you jump off a cliff, you will fall. Who you are, how much money you make, or what your belief system is, makes no difference. It is important that we understand how immutable laws like these work, so we can act intelligently. Ignorance of these laws can be quite dangerous.

What about other nonphysical laws like the *law of manifestation*? You might know it as "like attracts like" or "what you give you will receive" or "what goes around comes around" or "as ye sow, so shall ye reap." There are many descriptions in every country of this particular law. But, is this *law of manifestation* really a law and is it absolute? For insight, let's look to another law.

For decades I have heard of the *law of abundance*. This law states that there is enough of everything for everyone: enough food, enough love, enough of anything we could possible need or want. That *enough* never diminishes. There was enough two centuries ago; there is enough now; and there will be enough next year. Abundance for All! This spiritually based law is linked closely to the physical *Law of Conservation* that says in a closed system, the total quantity of something will not increase or decrease, but remain exactly the same.

Our planet could be considered a closed system of chemical properties. The quantity of these properties remains static even though they may change form. A tree may burn in the forest and it no longer exists as a tree. But, the chemical components that constructed the tree still exist, just in a different form. Those modified components are the stuff that fertilizes the ground and eventually grows a new tree, bush, or flower.

If abundance is the promise and nothing is ever lost to us, then why do so many of us experience lack? One way to examine this riddle is to recognize that even in an abundant reality, people can choose to consciously or unconsciously not see the abundance. If we stop questioning whether there is abundance and focus on how we do or do not use this law, we will find the reason for the experience of lack.

A reader discovered that she was an excellent manifestor of lack and that the roots of her skill went back to her upbringing. Once she recognized the law in action, she was able to redirect her aim and change her life.

"During the years my one daughter was a teenager, I was a single mom working full time and going to school at night to improve our lot in life. I began attending Unity Church and learned for the first time about the *universal law of prosperity*. In response to a number of lessons I heard presented there, I came to realize that I'd been focusing on lack, what I *didn't* have, and it had influenced almost everything I did: the clothes and makeup I bought, the food we purchased at a supermarket or a restaurant, our entertainment, my dreams . . . everything.

My mother was raised with five siblings as a poor child during the Great Depression. I think she passed on to my siblings and me the attitude that we weren't worth much; that we would never have enough, and that we would need to scratch out what we got. I accepted the attitude that I probably didn't deserve much. When considering the purchase of ANYthing, I always figured I couldn't afford it, didn't really need it, and certainly couldn't have it. I didn't believe that I could help anyone else with material things, certainly not with money, not even my church, where I'd been taught that ten percent of my income for tithing was expected. Somehow, I thought my circumstances didn't even qualify me for that expectation.

As a result of the *law of prosperity* first heard at Unity Church, I worked on my deservingness. I heard and began to believe that I was created good vs. being sinful, to be something, and to do something special. I learned to trust that I was worth more, and that I could have whatever I needed. I learned to give and trust that I would receive, that my needs would be fulfilled and that blessings would be returned to me. I learned (and continue to believe) that 'Divine Love blesses all that I have, all that I give, and all that I receive'—one of

Unity's affirmations repeated by the congregation during services.

I started giving more as offerings at church. At first it hurt. I was concerned that if I gave my earnings away, I would have less to purchase things we needed at home. Little by little, one thing at a time, I learned through practice that the more I gave, the more I received. I learned that as I gave 'love offerings,' I received more spiritual lessons. As I gave love away, I received more love. I learned that when I paid for car insurance and a good payment for a car, I had a nice car. I could be proud of the car I was driving. I saved myself the cost of repairs and the humility I'd been accustomed to feeling when driving the cheapest car I could find. I spent a little more money on my daughter and myself and wound up *having* more money to spend on things my daughter and I wanted. I learned I could buy gifts for other people and still have plenty of money to pay for my necessities. It felt good.

As I was learning this lesson of prosperity, I felt it was important to share this knowing with my daughter, so I announced to her one time, for the first time, that she didn't *have* to order the cheapest thing on the menu anymore. It was such a blessing to see the pleasure on her face, as she was able to experience the freedom of ordering whatever she wanted to order for the first time without considering the expense. Her attitude of abundance continues to this day as I observe my adult daughter purchasing what she desires, knowing that she *deserves* it.

Now in my sixties, I can buy whatever I need because I deserve it. I trust that there IS enough in the universe for us all to have what we need."—Dora Faye Hendricks

Even in a reality of plenty, our beliefs about whether we can personally manifest what we want determine our experience. If we believe that it is within our power to create the substance of our lives, we will consciously connect with our abundant reality and direct the fulfillment of our desires. If we believe that we are not in control of our experience of life, then we will still connect with our abundant reality. The critical difference between the two is that those who consciously connect with abundance will manifest what they want; those who unconsciously connect with abundance will manifest, but not necessarily what they want.

In truth, abundance doesn't promise happiness and wealth. It promises that there is *plenty* of everything for everyone: plenty of riches, plenty of poverty, plenty of health, and plenty of disease. We experience what we experience because of the companion law to the *law of abundance: the law of manifestation*. It states that if you plant corn you will manifest corn. The act and the result are inextricably linked like two ends of the same stick.

The act of will or manifestation *is* absolute. What we *will* to happen, will happen. But we must exert our will consciously. What we *say* we want is often not how we direct our minds or our actions. I can say I want to be wealthy, yet practice behaviors that lead to poverty. Saying is not manifesting. You must apply your conscious *will* to your words. Saying the words is the first step; willing the action is the second. Manifestation requires action.

To be even more exacting I can say I want abundance of wealth or happiness or love, yet deep down believe that it is not really possible for me. I believe in my doubt more than the possibility of goodness. And that, my friend, is where our manifestation energies go . . . into feeding what we believe is true for us. We get exactly what we plant: doubt and lack, just as the *law of manifestation* promises.

Now, here is an interesting twist. Every day that we experience lack is another day that proves that the *law of manifestation* and the *law of abundance* work. How so? We believe in our experience, in this case, a lack of money. That is a reality for us and all our thoughts are about that apparent lack. What we do not have and what we cannot afford are the thoughts we plant and that is the crop we reap—abundant lack. Because we are *telling* ourselves that we do not have enough, we manifest not enough to prove that our belief is right. We have a twisted sense that to be right is important, even to our detriment.

We may hate lack, but it is a positive demonstration of the *law of abundance* and the *law of manifestation*. We are incredible manifestors of lack, and misery, and confusion. To stop creating lack, we simply need to refocus intentions to the reality of plenty. We must stop planting lack if we wish to reap abundance.

How do we do this? We manage our thoughts. Whether consciously intended or unconsciously supported, our thoughts will result in the reality in which we believe.

What thoughts pass through your head every waking moment? Do you dwell on how sick you are, or how worried you are about meeting your financial obligations? Do you think about how lonely you are, or how much you hate your job, your spouse, and your life? Are these the seeds you plant each day? Are they the reality you are reinforcing and perpetuating?

If your answer to these questions is yes, rejoice! You have the *law of manifestation* mastered! Now simply adjust your aim. Turn your mind away from dwelling on what you don't want and focus instead on what you do want.

If you want to experience health, recognize how healthy you already are. Chances are whatever malady you may have, it is minor in proportion to your overall health. Are you financially strapped? Look at what you do have. It's likely that you are richer than the majority of people on the planet.

I am not saying to simply be thankful for what you already have and leave it at that. Being thankful for what you already have is acknowledging that you *can* manifest abundance. It is recognizing that the truth of abundance does exist in your life. When we recognize what we have already accomplished, it nourishes our belief that we can do more.

This abundance/lack issue is simply one of aim. The *law of manifestation* is at work all the time. If we are experiencing lack, we are letting our attention dwell on lack. We are making it *real*. Learning how to manage our thoughts is the key to planting the seeds we want to grow. If you find yourself living in the land of lack, stop your mind and say, "The truth is that there is more than enough for me. I am ready and willing to accept my rightful good."

Don't just make this a mindless affirmation. Saying the words will not cancel out the thought that you are faking it, if you are. You must *believe* your words. Remain conscious of what your self talk is. Unmanaged self talk tends to flow to the negative. Your job is to redirect it. Whenever you find yourself feeling depressed, stop and recognize your thoughts. Listen in . . . you will hear horrible prophesies and exaggerated disasters. None of this is true. It is just your mind running amok, not being managed.

Your mind is a tool, not a master. Step in and establish your conscious will and manifest the abundance you deserve and want! The real test of mind management is the conscious choice of our emotions. Unless we pay attention, we will often be at the effect of our involuntary emotions. As we've already seen, it's easy to let fear, doubt, and confusion set up camp and dictate what emotions we experience. But, you can manifest peace and happiness by redirecting your mind's focus. In the following chapter, we'll see how happiness can be your consistent state of being no matter what's going on in your life. In that state of being, you will enhance your ability to use the *law of abundance* and the *law of manifestation*.

14 I Choose Happy

"Happiness is inward and not outward;
and so it does not depend on what we have, but on what we are."
—Henry Van Dyke

Author's Note: Is it possible to be truly happy when your life is falling apart?
Learn how.

I want some new shoes, a bigger house, and a more romantic partner. I want more money, more time off, and more fun. The list is endless. I have a seemingly insatiable appetite for more of this and more of that. Like trying to fill a bottomless pit. It does not matter that my closet is filled with shoes I have barely worn or that I often forego interesting activities for the sake of a lame television sitcom. I look at what I have. I look at what is out there. And I want more. Don't you?

One day I came across this quote, as if it had been waiting for me to show up: "You won't be happy with more until you're happy with what you've got."—Viki King. Hmm, happy with what I've got. That is where I get stuck, somewhere between fulfillment and hunger, with hunger usually taking the lead.

It just seems that if I am happy with what I've got, more won't show up. Either my get-up-and-go will get up and go, or the universe will look in and see that I am satisfied where I am and pass me by with the next helping of the good life. Don't contented people stop trying? So, I discount what is mine and long for what is not mine.

In our American society, that hunger for more is totally encouraged. It is expected that you are unsatisfied with today, so that you will be motivated to get to tomorrow. Starter homes, used cars, base salaries are all just stepping stones to something bigger, better, and faster. And stepping quickly is the name of the game. Get there fast and grab as much as you can along the way. I believe the bumper sticker reads, "He who dies with the most toys, wins." Hundreds of commercials assault us daily with the message that more is better. Never be satisfied with what you have today, since you could have *much* more.

By constantly keeping our eyes on tomorrow's riches, we never appreciate the beauty, love, and bounty surrounding us today. *Stop and smell the roses*. We are surrounded with riches and abundance. Can we savor today's bounty without craving tomorrow's meal?

Beyond the battle for immediate or deferred happiness, this issue goes even deeper . . . into the core of what happiness is.

Is it possible to be really happy no matter what life dishes up? Where does happiness come from? From more stuff? From fulfilled dreams? We will be happy when such and such happens? This is a temporary happiness based on conditions.

The core of Ms. King's statement is that happiness is a choice, not a circumstance. It is not so much about being happy with what you have, as it is the choice to be happy, period. But, how can you be happy when your spouse has left you; when unpaid bills are stacking up; or when you've just lost your job? Happy?

Can we be happy just to be alive? Is this kind of happiness a bottom of the food chain version of happiness? Do we suffer in silence, not really believing we have a choice to be happy?

Can we, even in the worst of times, choose to be happy . . . without faking it? Theoretically, yes. But, we do not live in theory. When life is not how we wish it to be, can we still feel happiness? That question is one we each need to answer for ourselves. To have our state of mind be dependent upon life circumstances is to leave our happiness in the hands of everyone and everything else, but us.

Choosing to be happy when there is no obvious reason to be happy takes personal resolve and fortitude. It takes mental toughness and singular self-confidence. Happiness is a choice, not a chance.

It is not easy feeling contentment when we have just been hurt. Anger and resentment are more likely and might seem completely justified. Anger and resentment only hurt us further and push happiness beyond reach.

If I'm not happy now, will I ever be happy? If happiness truly does lie in my own hands, and I'm not happy now, then am I willing to believe it's in my control? If I believe instead that happiness is bestowed by what happens to me, then, yes, my life will always be ruled by circumstances.

Given Mary Anne's circumstances, her very life depended upon making a conscious choice for happiness.

"One year ago, my doctor called to tell me that I had melanoma (a form of skin cancer that can be deadly). My husband and I had just decided to start our family, but I wasn't pregnant yet. In a moment everything changed: my life, my outlook and perspective about every day work or personal issues.

After my diagnosis, I received LOTS of information from a specialty hospital regarding testing, surgery, future treatment plans, etc. My husband and I decided early on that we only wanted 'just in time information.' In other words, we wanted to have surgery to see if the cancer had spread to my lymph nodes before we learned what the treatment would be. I call this *taking life in small chunks*. Just live for today, and don't become overwhelmed with all the what ifs and buts.

You hear about so many people who have cancer, survived cancer and died of cancer. You can't imagine it until you receive the call.

After a lot of prayers, positive attitudes, and hopefulness, I am 100% cancer free with no need for any treatment other than surgery (removal). Amen! I also learned that a positive attitude does have a strong   impact   on   cancer   survivor   outcomes."
—Mary Anne Butz-Belanger

Of all the powers we have, the ability to choose what we experience through our mental and emotional states of being is the least developed and most essential power in leading a happy life. It is so easy to believe that true satisfaction is something we encounter, not something we create. But, you can develop this tool. Soon it will become an unconscious habit.

The first step is awareness. Are you conscious of when you are feeling unhappy? It is not hard to *feel* unhappy, but do you recognize how you are generating that feeling while it is happening? As sentient beings, we have a marvelous capacity to witness ourselves while we are *being* ourselves. To watch ourselves do; to think about our thinking. It is a form of personal observation. This separates us from lower life forms, this capacity for self-awareness.

When you feel yourself getting upset, imagine you are observing yourself from a distance . . . as if you are not you, but watching you. Notice what you do to fuel your disquiet. Do you behave in certain ways? Do you have specific facial expressions? Does the quality of your voice change? These responses to your feelings also intensify your feelings. Soon, the event that upset you to begin with becomes secondary to the response you are having to your feelings. Now you are engaged with your feelings, no longer the event itself.

When you can observe how you are responding to your feelings, you can begin to take control. Intellect begins to govern emotions. You can ask the question, "Is my response to this helping or hurting me?" Choice is restored. From gaining some perspective and stepping out of the overwhelming emotions, you can decide how to best achieve what you want; to decide how you want to feel.

In the early stages of honing this skill, this exercise in self-direction might feel a bit artificial. Purposefully managing our actions and reactions through conscious choice can feel awkward at first, but it will soon feel natural. Truthfully, you have been doing this all along. You just have not been aware of it. Every emotion you have is a choice that you make, consciously or unconsciously. The real satisfaction lies in choosing your state of mind, not reflexively reacting like an animal.

Your will is strong, if you exercise it. You can feel how you want to feel at any time you choose. The key is awareness. Happiness is, and always has been, your natural state. When you consciously choose, you will never choose or experience anything but happiness, because inside of you is true greatness, as our next chapter will reveal.

15 Greatness

> "You have powers you never dreamed of. You can do things you never thought you could do. There are no limitations in what you can do except the limitations of your own mind."
> —Darwin P. Kingsley

Author's Note: What will your legacy be? Learn to break through personal boundaries to discover your own greatness..

My city just celebrated the thirtieth anniversary of the opening of its 1974 World's Fair & Expo. Then, a little known town of 150,000 railroad workers, miners, ranchers, and farmers rose from obscurity to put Spokane, Washington, in the world's spotlight. Competing against prominent cities from all over the globe, the improbable victory of little Spokane was remarkable.

Reflecting the same spirit of determination, PBS-TV recently featured a documentary of the construction of the famous Golden Gate Bridge in San Francisco, California. *The Symphony in Steel* told of the bridge's troubled inception. Conceived in the 1920s by Joseph Strauss, the international orange, not golden, bridge met with instant opposition from the local ferry system, the Department of Defense, environmental groups, and lords of commerce. Each threw their enormous weight against this change. Because of the massive resistance, coupled with the country's economic depression, the bonds offered to raise the millions it would take to build the bridge would not sell. The bridge's completion seemed doomed, yet it majestically stands today.

At the completion of his mighty bridge, Joseph Strauss penned an impressive ode that he entitled "The Mighty Task Is Done." It epitomizes his personal travail in building the bridge and makes of the structure almost a living thing. From his poem, these lines give evidence of the dedication of the man who brought to life the bridge from his passionate vision.

> At last the mighty task is done;
> Resplendent in the western sun;
> The Bridge looms mountain high
> On its broad decks in rightful pride,
> The world in swift parade shall ride
> Throughout all time to be.
> Launched midst a thousand hopes and fears,
> Damned by a thousand hostile sneers.
> Yet ne'er its course was stayed.
> But ask of those who met the foe,

Who stood alone when faith was low,
Ask them the price they paid.
High overhead its lights shall gleam,
Far, far below life's restless stream,
Unceasingly shall flow. . . .

Total dedication and astonishing achievements like these renew my faith in man's enduring will. It lifts my heart and strengthens my own resolve to be more. We too easily forget, in the smallness of our daily tasks and responsibilities that humanity is meant for such daring and greatness.

"Karen has given me the vision to go out and challenge myself to see what I may be missing. I make myself go beyond what I think I'm able to do and color outside the lines. I would not have done this before I found Karen's heart in every word. Now I move toward the unknown with a passion for growth I've never had before. I've made the choice to face what it is that I fear, love, hate—and pay attention to it and do something about it." —Shari Penhall

In the span of human evolution, mankind has cured diseases that otherwise would have ended millions of human lives. Not only have we broken the bonds of gravity, we've flown to other planets. Nations that have endured a lineage of brutal dictators have ended generations of oppression to assume the rights and responsibilities of freedom. We have created amazing technology that lets a rice paddy farmer in China speak to an ice fisherman in Norway.

To forget our inborn greatness is only half living. Small lives are not our divine destiny. With the largest brains (relative to body size) on the planet, we are the only species to participate in and guide our own evolution. As we have progressed, we have cultivated values, ethics, and a consciousness to transform our very world.

We have the gifts of creativity, imagination, and courage. We can look beyond what *is* to what *can be*. We can dream and dream big!

There is still much to do in this world. Globally, diseases still kill millions. Ninety percent of the African continent suffers from AIDS. Countless masses are still oppressed. Many third-world countries still have no elected governments, nor rights and freedoms for their peoples. And as far as it has come in such a short time, technology is still just a fledgling gadget that has not yet reached its ultimate potential.

Each day the demands of an ever accelerating pace of life generate more and more responsibilities. Some days we are running like a blur from one commitment to another. But, though we can be distracted by the mundane, somewhere along the way, we must remember that we are all capable of extraordinary things.

What will be our era's legacy? What will we leave behind that proclaims to future generations that we left this world in better shape than we found it? Will we be the ones to discover a new cure to a ravaging disease? Will we become the leaders of tomorrow, blazing the way to freedom for all humankind? Will our research in the field of biotechnology free the human body to regenerate needed organs or replace missing limbs? These are not impossible legacies, but instead, a defiance of mediocrity that echoes the longing of our souls to matter—to make a difference—to be the magnificence we are meant to be.

Pause for a moment and envision what *your* legacy will be. Will this world be a better place because you have lived? Will you have given more than you took? Did your contribution lighten the burden of another? In the final moments, will you close your eyes and know that your life had truly mattered?

I, too, forget the astonishing blessing that is my life: to breathe and think and do—to love and forgive and trust. This gift of life we have each received is not ours alone. How pointless to be born and die and in between serve only our little egos. Magnificence! That is why we are here. Doesn't the word itself make you sit taller and breathe deeper? *Be* magnificent and *do* wondrous things. Never doubt that the seeds of greatness lay dormant within you. It is your divine destiny.

When one of Sonja Meline's students was casually discarded as a failure by school authorities, she chose to act on what she knew to be his inherent magnificence. This is her story.

"I'm a School and Home Interventionist on a Native American Reservation in North Dakota. It's a hard job, but I love every one of these kids. I can understand them, because I was raised to be a victim myself. *Don't rock the boat. Don't make anybody angry. Everybody else is more important.* These are the voices I heard for forty years living in fear, because I was raised as a wimp. I married somebody who was constantly beating me down. But, I eventually found out that I'm not a wimp—I am a warrior! I finally broke out of the victim box. And it's been an interesting ride.

Poverty is horrible on this reservation. Drugs and alcohol are real problems, as is physical and sexual abuse. It's tough. It's hard for these kids. They aren't told that they're wonderful. A lot of times they come to school without breakfast. They might not have eaten the night before, either, or they had a bag of chips or something. One kid hid out in the woods all night because his dad came home drunk and beat his mom. This is their reality—neglect.

In working with these kids, I was very honest about my fears and my feelings. They were surprised that they weren't alone in feeling like they did. Everyone needs encouragement. You need the pat on the back or kick in the butt just to know that you're not the only one out there having trouble. You're not the only person that is misunderstood.

I taught in a psych hospital and one of my students was a sixth grade kid. He was depressed and had just tried to commit suicide. He'd been higher than a kite when they did a psychological test on him, and he came up as mildly retarded. When he came into my classroom I started with the obvious. He's a sixth grader, so I tried sixth grade math.

He took the math book and threw it at my head! He said, 'I can do that in my f_____ sleep.'

I said, 'Okay, if you know all that, let's try pre-algebra.' The kid was amazing. He went through Pre-algebra, Algebra I and II in four months. He was a genius! He was just bored out of his mind in school. He was depressed, not stupid. And he wasn't retarded.

He drew a picture for me that looked like it was coming right out at me off the paper. I said, 'Oh, this is really cool. How did you do this?'

He wrote down a mathematical equation and said, 'This is my formula.'

I asked him if he realized his drawing looked like a time warp going into a black hole. He had no idea what I was talking about, so I took him to my office to find my college science book. I opened up the page and said, 'This is your picture, isn't it?'

He was dumbfounded. His picture was looking back at him from a college science textbook. Right after that he made a fairly functional black hole for the science fair. Considering he was a sixth grader, taking second place was quite an achievement.

I administered an aptitude test on him myself. This time he tested off the chart. I collected all kinds of things he'd done and my test results and went back to the administration to tell them he needed to be retested. The mildly retarded label was wrong, and the school needed to make it right.

They told me that in a perfect world one could get whatever one wanted, but not here. He'd already been tested and the score would stand as is.

I was livid! I left the meeting and went straight to the boy. I told him what had happened in the meeting. 'Do you want to know who I think you are?'

He looked up and stared straight into my eyes.

I said, 'You are Michelangelo. You are Leonardo da Vinci. You are Albert Einstein. You are Galileo. Do you know what these guys were?'

He replied, 'What?'

'These guys were original thinkers. These men were made fun of. These men didn't quite fit in. They were so far out of the norm that regular people just couldn't figure out what was going on with these guys! But, where would we be without them? You are in that category. You belong there. The ball is in your court. You can just sink right down to the depths of despair and you can become a bum in the street, or you can take your God given right and your God given brains and do something with them.'

Well, the kid graduated. The last I heard he was in a highly accelerated program in Wyoming.

Karen, I keep going back to your e-zines. That's what happens. That's what you provide. It's a touchstone. It's a foot up. It's an, *I'm not crazy. I'm not alone.* We are all capable of so much, if we just believe in ourselves and stop deferring to everyone else's opinions."
—Sonja Meline

Sonja saw her student's greatness when everyone else was willing to write him off as a lost cause. She proclaims that there is much more to each of us than our momentary circumstances or behavior might indicate.

Look up from the details of your day occasionally and see life with fresh eyes. Find your place in the world's symphony and play your instrument loudly and passionately. You are not dispensable; you don't sit second chair to anyone. The world needs your song desperately. Do not be whom Oliver Wendell Holmes spoke of in his famous quote, "Many of us go to our graves with our music still inside us."

You are here for a reason. Find out what yours is. This is your time to shine. It is not only your privilege, but also your responsibility to humankind to contribute your gifts to this world.

The focus of the section we're concluding, The Fires Come, has been aimed at exploring and developing the spiritual skills to withstand your personal challenges. Challenges that test your level of awareness and beliefs about yourself and the world. Facing such difficulties burns away all that is erroneous and may distract you from the task you are here to live: the fulfillment of your purpose. Revisit these chapters often. Personal growth is an evolution that requires patience and persistence. Now is not the time to rush. Your inner sense of peace will reveal to you when it's time for you to move on.

Beginning with Chance the Rapids, we will move into the final section of *The Sequoia Seed*: The Mighty Sequoia Grows. These final chapters will examine the unfolding and ripening of your purpose and path. With the skills from this section in hand, we'll look at how to follow your heart and resolve your will. We'll also celebrate living on purpose and remember what's most valued in this journey to wholeness.

Act Three:

The Mighty Sequoia Grows

-fulfilling your promise

# 16 Chance the Rapids

"Twenty years from now you will be more disappointed by the things that you didn't do than by the ones you did do. So throw off the bowlines. Sail away from the safe harbor. Catch the trade winds in your sails. Explore. Dream. Discover."
—Mark Twain

Author's Note: Are your days filled with empty details while your dream withers? Don't miss out on your life. It's not too late to wake up.

Years ago, one of country singer Garth Brook's songs reached into a secreted place within me and touched a yearning that I didn't realize existed. It was something primal and compelling. The song was *The River*. It speaks of living deliberately and fighting the pull to just drift along. My heart responded in one frightful leap to his prophetic words: "choose to chance the rapids, dare to dance the tides." It's funny how truth reaches out and grabs you. As a reminder to stay conscious, I emblazoned the sentiment on a license plate holder and mounted it on the rear bumper of my 4Runner. Whenever I saw it, time and again, I remembered, "Don't slide through life. Make this day count."

Occasionally I noticed drivers in cars stopped behind me at traffic lights, straining to read the message. Some looked confused, but others smiled, getting its metaphoric meaning. Secretly I hoped that the sting of those words would strike at the hearts of all who saw them.

In a life where one day tends to blend seamlessly into the next, it's easy to just drift along, to go with the flow, not make waves, and to leave little trace of our existence. We can get hypnotized by the endlessness of minutes and hours and days. Time seems eternal. Another tomorrow follows this day like clockwork. It is so easy to sleep through life . . . so comfortable to slip into habit and routine. Soft, warm, familiar . . .

WAKE UP!

"The sun will come out tomorrow . . . " is *not* a promise, it's simply an expectation, and expectations are shattered all the time. At some point, when it's too late for you to do anything about it, tomorrow *won't* come. Time *will* run out. The last thing you did will forever be the *last* thing you did.

Truly, today is all you have—this minute—this moment. Don't fall asleep and miss out on your life. To assume that you will have tomorrow to do what you did not do today is to, one day, miss your chance. Today is all you can count on.

Keep what's most important in your life front and center. The so-called urgent tasks and niggling to-dos will not fulfill you, no matter how long your list. Yet, we tend to measure our productivity by checking those tasks off of our list. Ironically, it seems that the more insignificant the task, the greater the chance that it will get done. Why? Because it is easy and doesn't require much of us. It also doesn't usually add up to much either, but hey . . . it got checked off.

It's the non-urgent stuff that most often gets postponed. Telling your loved ones how fortunate you are to have them in your life. Saying "I'm sorry" for the stupid thoughtless thing you said that upset a friend. Calling the company you'd really like to work for, to see if there is an opening. Visiting your lonely grandfather in his retirement community. Taking time to stroll around the park, even once, to remember what it feels like to have the warm sun on your face. Stopping, for a moment, to remember the passion you harbor for an almost forgotten dream.

What truly matters most in our lives seems to go unattended, day after day, year after year. We immerse ourselves in the quantity of our days and neglect the quality of our lives. But, it's not too late to stop the neglect, and it's never too early to make up for lost time. Today *can* be different. It only takes a different decision.

Teresa looked at her life and realized that she was living her days doing work that meant less and less to her, while her family and passions took a backseat. So she decided to resurrect a childhood passion and focus her life on her real values.

"Growing up with six other brothers and sisters in a three bedroom home was delightful, most of the time, and cozy to say the least. I often found myself in need of space—a retreat. In the summer months this was not a problem for there was lots of outdoors in which to get away. In the winter months I designed the perfect spaces in corners of rooms or in our unfinished basement. One winter I claimed the space under the stairs as my territory and it became my personal haven.

Since that time long ago, I have consistently found myself recreating space, especially neglected space, like the historic homes I now restore.

The first home I purchased was an old school house in Logan, Utah. After much labor, it was a beautiful home with unmatched character. I fell in love with the whole process of taking something so neglected and turning it into something so special. The process of renewing hidden wood flooring is likely the most emotionally impressive. After that, I was hooked and decided to make this my full time profession.

I'd worked in the corporate world in Human Resources and Training. My job gave me limited time for my family and social life, let alone my many projects. Aching to do restorations full time and create a way to sustain our family financially through my passion became a constant in my life. After much hesitation I went under, over, and through! I now restore, at minimum, two historic homes or properties per year and have managed to spend the majority of my time with my family. What a blessing vision is, what an illusion ego is.

Several old homes later I found myself on my hands and knees listening, as I would rip away layers of floor covering (carpet, linoleum, paint), and it was as though I could feel the wood breathe. And as I revealed the wood floor beneath, I felt as though I was also *de-layering*. There was such a sense of gratitude on both ends at that very moment.

As much as I love this, I have moments where it's completely exhausting and I wonder if I'm nuts doing this. It's been scary at times along the way because sometimes I don't know how the finances are going to work and how it's going to turn out. There have been several times when I've contemplated going back to work, even in order to make something happen and it just seems like the more faith I put into this work and the more I let go, the more I'm given what I need to make it happen. So, I'm encouraged.

This is where my heart is. And it serves a great purpose. I see the people that come into these homes and they just absolutely love them! The home that we just sold was so hard for me to let go of emotionally. My husband has *wanted* me to sell it for a long time and I really, for some reason, emotionally connected with this home. I finally let go emotionally and, of course, we sold it that week. I could feel the energy of the home in gratitude to me. I knew that it was my time to go. It was fabulous, the people that came forth. It was just like a happy ending even though it involves a house! It's the simplicity of a house. I just feel that energy there and it's wonderful to experience that."
—Teresa Nelson

Just for today resurrect your dream. Do *one* thing that breathes life into its parched lungs. Call your friend and mend the fence. Be sure that the last words you say to a loved one before you part are, "I love you." It may be the last words they ever hear you speak.

Choose to *chance the rapids*—it is in the churn of life where dreams are born. *Dare to dance the tides*—be bold in your actions. Savor the sour and the sweet. Live the highs and lows. Feel it all. That is what your senses are for! Take it in, in huge gulps and give it back in armloads. Feel the flow of life rushing through your veins.

On my birthday several years back, I felt disturbingly disconnected from life when I realized that too many of my years had been spent drifting. I didn't have what I had thought I would have had by that point. I hadn't had the adventures I'd always dreamed of. I wasn't yet the person I'd hoped to become. Looking back, I didn't like the meager existence I had chosen. Looking ahead, I realized that I had less time than I'd already wasted. A sobering thought.

I wondered how much time I might still have left to turn my life around. Many, many years, I hoped. But, we do not live in years, we live in days. So, I calculated how many days I might yet live. The life expectancy for a healthy white woman living in the United States at that time was seventy-eight years. I was forty at the time. More than halfway there. So, I subtracted forty from seventy-eight and multiplied that number by three hundred sixty-five days in a year.

I expected to see a really large number. I stared in disbelief at the calculator and at the frighteningly small number of my potentially remaining days—only 13,870!

I looked back on how I had spent the day before and could not really remember anything I did of worth. I thought about the half year that had just passed and realized that it had slipped by almost without notice. I thought about the years of my past where I could not recall even one memory. I had lived 14,600 days and it seemed to add up to very little. I had to wake up! The day was almost gone; the year was half gone. I had to pay attention and live my life as if it mattered!

Fight the deadness of inertia with all your might. Do not fall asleep! Not even for a minute. It may be your last. You wouldn't want to miss it, would you? Listen to your heart. Is it suffocating as you go about *business as usual*?

Right now, this minute, break the chains of your routine and do something totally out of character, totally life affirming. Dare to live deliberately on this planet. Will yourself to live fully. Make this day the only one you have and a day of triumph over monotony. The moment you do, the spell will be broken and you will wonder why you ever settled for less. *And* you will never settle for less again.

Each of us in life will receive a chance to do something truly remarkable. Will you be ready? Will your resolve to *chance the rapids* give you the strength to meet the challenge? In the next chapter, I confess to a moment of weakness when my desire to live fully succumbed to my fear and doubt. I remember it as one of those moments that could have been life changing, but I let it go. I do regret that.

17 Dancing with Destiny

"The roads we take are more important than the goals we announce.
Decisions determine destiny."
—Frederick Speakman

*Author's Note: Learn how to identify the sound of your inner voice and recognize
the divine clues that you've been missing.*

Life is a journey and sometimes you come to a crossroads where one decision will forever change the direction of your life. This was that day for me.

A friend asked if I could give her a ride to work because her car was in the shop. I was glad for the company on my normally solitary commutes across the infamous Golden Gate Bridge and into San Francisco, California. After a brief pause in our chitchat, my friend declared that her sister had "up and quit her job." It seemed she and a friend had decided to start a tour company.

The fact that neither of them had experience in the travel industry was evidently not a deterrent. My friend was astonished at such a rash decision, but I was enchanted by the courage it took to embark on such a spontaneous and extraordinary venture.

All that morning my thoughts kept drifting back to that conversation. Something about the oh-my-God-ness of it all haunted me. Lunchtime found me walking to the library without a real plan of any kind. I just felt a need to explore. An itch had begun that demanded to be scratched.

It seemed perfectly logical to start with the A's at the card catalog. My flipping fingers stopped when they reached East Africa. I stared at the card and the sub-titles of Kenya and Tanzania. I had no idea where Kenya was or what it was like, but somewhere deep in my belly a hole began to open up—one of those black holes that threatens to swallow up everything comfortable and normal.

In that moment, staring at that card, I began a ravenous obsession with Africa that defied all logic. I read all of Isak Dinesen's books of her African adventures. Meryl Streep played her character in the movie *Out of Africa*; a single woman pitting herself and her future as a coffee farmer against the hardships of early twentieth century Kenya. I bought and memorized every word and scene of that movie! When Meryl spoke, I felt the words coming from my own mouth.

I also discovered and fell in love with Beryl Markham in her autobiography *West with the Night*. Beryl was born in 1902 and emigrated to East Africa with her father. He chose East Africa because, "it was new and you could feel the future of it under your feet." The genes of adventure coursed through Beryl's veins as well, because in 1936 she became the first person to fly an east to west solo across the Atlantic, surviving a crash landing in Nova Scotia twenty-one hours and twenty-five minutes after take off from London.

I immersed myself in all things Kenyan. I studied Swahili. I researched the politics of the region, its culture, and its struggles as a growing third-world country. I read about the wildlife and was mesmerized by the romance of living so close to such raw beauty. I was hopelessly spellbound and I didn't know why.

It's hard to articulate the overpowering pull of this kind of internal magnetic urge. Without question I *knew* I must move to East Africa. Not visit, not dream about—MOVE THERE! Every cell in my body screamed this at me every day for months. But, rather than follow this calling, I questioned it. How could I just leave? I knew no one in Africa. I didn't have enough money. What would I do there? How would I live? Where would I live? How would I make money? What if I didn't like it? What if . . . what if . . . what if?

Slowly and methodically I killed the dream inside me. Its death came at the hands of my doubts and fears and my unwillingness to trust the voice within me. Never before had I felt a hunger so powerful and so incomprehensible pulling me toward the unknown. But, I didn't go. I let my fears win.

There's a part of me, when I let it have a voice, which knows beyond doubt that I was being called to play in a reality bigger than my solitary life. Although I wasn't privy to it at the time, there was something there in Kenya that I was supposed to do: a destiny that I was meant to fulfill. But I didn't, because I was afraid.

I may never know the course my life might have taken had I possessed the courage of Isak or Beryl to follow a dream. Part of me mourns losing my dream of Africa. I wonder if I will ever again have the chance to feel such a profound compulsion—a chance to ride the wind and trust.

Tracey Hill and her husband met and conquered their fears and walked into the unknown to start a new life. Here's her story.

"Like many people, I was raised to be a good, obedient girl, and to gain approval by behaving according to the expected standards. I was told I could do anything I set my mind to, but really approval came only from making the *correct* choices. Approval and support were withheld when I made *incorrect* choices. *Make the right choices, live the right way, and all will be well*, the unspoken messages seemed to say.

So, I went to college, made prudent career path choices, and fifteen years later looked in the mirror and wondered whose life I really was living. I was capable at my job and enjoyed some aspects of it, but mostly felt that I was slowly suffocating. I looked around the conference table at a meeting one day, and realized that the people I'd worked with for so many years were all now decidedly grey at the temples, and yet we were all still there, doing what, exactly? And why?

Gradually, I began to feel more and more that my life no longer fit me (if it ever really had). But my life was familiar, and the comfort of that familiarity was, oh, so seductive. . . .

Three years ago, my husband and I decided to take a gamble and leave the congested suburbs of Southern California for a new life and new opportunities in the Pacific Northwest. We went with our plans for the future somewhat unformed, trusting that we would find jobs and new friends and everything that we would need. Prudent? Definitely NOT! Letting go of the sense of security provided by a steady job with benefits and risking everything to start afresh was one of the scariest things I've ever done.

I was afraid, at first, to tell people what we were doing, expecting to be blasted by everyone for stepping out of line, not conforming, making a leap into a very uncertain future. What amazed me was that we got almost none of that. In fact, most of the people we spoke with actually sounded rather wistful, as though they too wished to break free, but were afraid to try, or believed it was impossible.

It's been a difficult three years, as we've struggled with unemployment, severely diminished income, dwindling savings, family problems, depression and fear. Our timing turned out not to be so good, but we could not have anticipated the tragedy of September 11th, and the effect it would have on jobs and the economy.

The dreams we had of an easy transition to our new life have not yet come true, but it's also been a time of tremendous growth, discovery and strengthening. I've had to face my fears of loss and lack head-on, and just about every fear I've ever harbored has crawled out at one time or another, large as any monster lurking in a child's closet at night.

But I haven't died of fear after all, and I've learned that even though I may be scared, the fears don't have to govern my life anymore. We've found wonderful people, marvelous experiences, and I've learned that I can survive more than I thought possible—things I might never have learned had we decided to play it safe.

Through the dark days and the joyful ones, the 'Waking Up' messages have provided a beacon of hope, inspiration and support, often bringing me words of hope when I had none left of my own to cling to. Frequently they spoke exactly the words I needed to hear in that moment, relating directly to the struggle I was then facing. They've provided me with reminders of what is important: insight, clarity, and food for thought, including (or perhaps especially) when the message required a look into the mirror at something I didn't really care to see.

So was I foolhardy to throw prudence to the wind and pursue a rather nebulous dream? Probably. Would I do it again, if I knew then what I know now? Honestly, it depends on what day you ask me. I still have my up days and my down ones. Is it necessary for everyone to throw their current life in the wastebasket and start over in order to find freedom of spirit? Definitely not! But it is necessary to wake up and really look at your life, at what is and isn't fulfilling your needs, and then take action to create a life that fits the you that you are now, not who you were, or who others want you to be, and to leave some room in that life for your spirit to continue to grow and expand."—Tracy H.

As Tracy discovered, stepping into the unknown isn't always easy and probably *never* is. It requires strong faith and resolve. It will challenge everything you've ever believed about life and yourself. It will strip away your sleepy existence and demand that you wake up. Changes of this magnitude are a rebirth, wrenching you from a stagnant life and launching you into a new reality.

But, as intense as this sounds, this step is as necessary for your life as the air you breathe. This level of calling only comes when you, consciously or unconsciously, have drawn it to yourself. Your spirit knows when it's time to move on. Not for the changes you'll encounter in your new world, but for the essential internal growth you must experience to make the contribution you came here to make. Like the caterpillar in the chrysalis, you are undergoing a transformation to prepare you for the life to come.

Perhaps you too have stopped momentarily at a crossroads. Perhaps you have been drawn toward the obscure path and wrestled with your own doubts. Maybe you are there right now. Will you have the courage to step forward? Will you trust divine direction? How might that make all the difference in the life you call your own?

"So, here I am. I still have my rumpled, crumpled, coffee stained copy of Run for the Roses, and I have found my rose. The best thing I've found here is a sense of peace I've never felt before. I've found that packing up and moving is overwhelming and frightening, but I CAN do it.

I have learned a lot about myself. I no longer NEED others to help me. I know what is inside of me. I've learned to make do or do without, and I learned never, never use your cruise control in a blizzard!

Would I do it again? In one skinny minute. I just regret wasting all the years I listened to certain members of my family belittle and tear apart my dreams and ambitions. I regret it took me so long to find my backbone and do what I wanted to do, whether anyone believed in me or not."
—Kathleen Messick

When the moment is presented to leap forward, hesitation can kill your chance and your spirit. In our next chapter, Run for the Roses, we consider whether the potential you harbor within you has a shelf life. Will it always be there or, when you finally accept the call, will the potential to respond be gone?

18   Run for the Roses

"Live not as though there were a thousand years ahead of you.
Fate is at your elbow; make yourself good while life and power are still yours."
—Marcus Aurelius

Author's Note: What if everything you want, wants you too?
How might that transform your life?

In a world too often filled with inane rhetoric and empty words, music pierces the heart with a *raw* poignancy of truth and beauty. Joyous or sorrowful, music speaks a language known to every ear. It is the catalyst of emotion and the memory of our most elemental knowing. Every ritual and ceremony throughout human evolution has called upon music to move the senses and declare import. Music makes us *feel*. It enlivens us.

In a brief three minutes, a song can say what eons cannot. Upon occasion, it can exhume something within us so profound that our lives are forever changed. I am often unreasonably touched by music, by lyrics that expose our common human frailty or a haunting melody that rushes over me like a tidal wave. Music has a way of bypassing the logic of our minds to delve deep into raw emotion. Music is our connection with eternal truths.

This I have found with Dan Fogelberg's *Run for the Roses*. Though sung about a young colt destined to become a champion racehorse, Dan's words also speak to the inherent potential in us all. They speak to the chance of a lifetime when we can soar higher and touch the fulfillment we're here to feel. I experience a mix of exhilaration and torment in hearing their truth. For deep inside, where I dare not peer too long, I know that I have not yet lived the life I am here to know. I have not yet trusted that my dreams are meant to live. Perhaps you know what I mean.

Each of us tenderly cradles our unborn dreams, secretly amazed at the promise, yet terrified of the price. Caught between desire and fear, we hesitate and hope and waste away wanting a guarantee of success. The only surety in life is: that which we breathe life into *will* live. Would you have it any other way? The elegance is pure. Action, not potential, begets results.

Fate delivers to us windows of opportunity when all is in place for us to take action. Sometimes that window of opportunity is open for only a brief moment. Does that mean our chance is gone? Does potential have a shelf life? No, potential is eternal, but it cannot bloom in soil rife with fear. So, it waits patiently for us to choose differently; to recognize how powerful we really are; to simply *join in the dance of life.* Sometimes it waits for an eternity.

Donna didn't wait forever. She looked at her life and realized she wanted more.

"In 1998, because of a series of events, I finally realized I was wasting my life away waiting for the children to grow up so I could get out of a dysfunctional relationship and get on with my life. So I packed up my car with my Jergens® lotion (funny what gives you a feeling of home and security) and a few other items and drove across the George Washington Bridge to Pennsylvania and a new beginning. We don't always leave gracefully, and there is no good way out of a marriage. It was the hardest, most crazy, and strengthening times of my life.

I lived for six months out of a suitcase on $6,000, that I had scraped together from my craftwork. When the divorce was finalized, I got a house close to where my children were living, and a job nearby, working as a nanny My children stayed with me two weeks out of every month. I felt like I was a large ship that had just ridden through a storm. I needed to find some balance and some stability, which I finally did.

After a while I realized that again, I was just existing and not following my dream. I wanted to help people to heal. So I decided to take a risk and registered for massage therapy school. I was working part time, some weeks making only $120, but I knew I had to follow my dream now or it would never happen. Mind you, I was forty-eight years old and the fear demons were alive and yelling, 'What if I'm too old to learn? What if I'm too old for the physical work? What if I can't pay the loans each month? What if I don't pass the tests? Blah . . . blah . . . blah.' I did it anyway.

Today, four years later, and after two years of working sixty-hour weeks without a day off, I can tell you that it was the best move I ever made. Every road I took, whether a side road, or supposedly a mistaken road, they all helped me make it here. I am now working about twenty or less hours a week in my own business out of a New Age store doing massage and supporting myself and my two children very comfortably." –Donna C.

It's easy for us to postpone life and wait until we feel confident that it will all turn out perfectly. We wait too willingly—to our own detriment. We think we are not ready. We think failure will be worse than the steady decay of delay. We think it does not really matter if we bloom in this life or wilt on the vine. But, what could matter more? We have been given a gift of exquisite possibility, yet we treat it like a cheap trinket. What magnificence we discount!

You must recognize by now, if you have been reading my work for any length of time, that you are eavesdropping on my own self-counseling. The fact that you make it to the conclusions of my writings is an indication that you are familiar with the path I walk. Perhaps you are asking the same questions and struggling with similar challenges. So, what do we do now with this persistent procrastination of potential promise?

I will give you my most cherished glimpse of wisdom. Are you ready? It will change your life forever! Here you go: "*GET OVER IT!*" Isn't there a part of you that is just plain sick of waiting and wondering? A part that just simply wants to get on with it? Have you considered that maybe there is nothing more we need to figure out? That there is nothing we need to do to be more ready? That just maybe, the real secret to living a life of fulfillment and meaning is to choose to do so and not stop choosing?

What if all our longing for what we think is beyond our grasp is due to our own blindness? What if everything we yearn for wants us too? What if all the barriers and obstacles and taboos we have *imagined* surrounding our deepest desires *are* just that—imagined? What if the cards really are stacked in our favor, but we have just never finished a hand?

Doesn't this ring true? I know it does for me. Every now and then I get just plain disgusted with my hesitancy and pitiful fear. Now is one of those times, hence, this writing.

We seem to have a gift of seeing in others the very things we try so hard to hide in ourselves. It is life's way of getting through our denial to deliver messages portending personal change. Sarah was the vehicle for a message I needed badly to hear. I knew Sarah years ago and always admired her ability to really connect with people. She had such ease and poise. People were attracted to her lively spirit and she showed such promise. Everyone sensed a greatness lying dormant within her. I know I did. Sarah was one of those predawn stars blazing in the sky. You just knew that, when her time came, she would go far in life.

But, when opportunity after opportunity came knocking, Sarah would hesitate. She would doubt herself and worry that she would not live up to the expectations others had of her. And they *did* have great expectations. She confided in me that if she tried and failed, she would not be able to face their disappointment. What I also suspected was that if she failed, she would not be able to face the loss of the promise.

Sarah had everything going for her, but confidence. Everyone knew she could set the world afire. She could write her own ticket. But, she never did. All that potential . . . unused.

Sure, she has a good life and those who don't know her well might never know of her inner disappointment. But, I do. I have heard her utter the words, "What if I had . . ." too many times. She was frozen by her fear years ago but hangs onto the *promise* of possibility by an ever-thinning thread. Possibility that may never be known if she continues to cherish the promise of a fulfilled life more than the reality of one. Does potential have a shelf life? As surely as all else, it will expire when we do.

We live in a miraculous world of plenty. If it is not plentiful in your own back yard, you have feet, move! We have magnificent minds and strong spirits. Imaginations so powerful that we can make up an impotent fantasy like fear and then pretend it dominates us. That is all fear is, imagined. It is the mind's response when it is unsure. Ninety-nine percent of the fear that paralyzes us simply does not exist outside our minds.

So, there you have it. It is all in our minds: fear, desire, doubt, and promise. Each day, each moment, we cast a vote for emotion that will rule us. Will we choose to cower or charge? The choice is ours, and only ours, each day, every day.

Let's make a pact. Let's let our hopes and dreams have at least equal time. Let's realize that they are just as potent as any concocted boogieman. That our aspirations are just as real and possible as our fears. Which of these will live, depends upon which one we choose. It always has been about our choices, and it will always be about our choices. It is all there for us. All we have to do is reach. Wouldn't you know it? We just happen to have two arms!

In Pushing the Wrong Rock, our next chapter, we'll learn that not all choices are life-long paths. Sometimes we'll discover we're going in the wrong direction in our lives and need to make a course correction. How do you do that when your whole life is built around the direction you're headed? It's not impossible. The alternative is too horrible to even contemplate.

19 Pushing the Wrong Rock

"Success requires first expending ten units of effort to produce one unit of results.
Your momentum will then produce ten units of results with each unit of effort."
—Charles Givens

Author's Note: Is this the life you had imagined you'd be living?
It's never too late to change directions.

The little boy had been warming the bench all season; watching his teammates run up and down the court scoring baskets and blocking shots. But, he did not complain or lose hope. He cheered his team with endless enthusiasm. Every basket was a victory and every turnover was a disappointment. His body might not have been in the game, but his heart sure was!

It was the last game of the season and the clock ticked away the final minutes of play. His team's winning season was about to be capped with a run-away victory against their arch rival. Suddenly, the words he had longed to hear, "Jeff, you're up." His heart began to race as Coach pointed to an open position on the floor.

Jeff dashed clumsily to take his spot, a big smile beaming from his face. He knew all the plays; he had been watching carefully for months. One of his mates rebounded a wild shot and passed the ball directly to him. With no hesitation, Jeff took off like a rocket!

Suddenly, he heard his coach's voice, "Jeff, you're dribbling the ball the wrong way!"

"I know," Jeff shouted over his shoulder, but he kept running. Again the coach tried to correct his player's course. And, again, Jeff responded with an insistent, "I know!"

Waving his arms wildly now, the coach hollered, "Hey, Jeffrey, you are going the wrong way!"

Jeff, equally exasperated, shouted back, "I KNOW! I CAN'T TURN THE BALL AROUND!"

Amusing story, but poignant message. How many times in your life you have dribbled the wrong way? Said yes when you wanted to say no. Remained silent when you wanted to ask. Stayed when you wanted to leave. The pull of inertia is powerful. Once you establish a way of being, it can feel almost impossible to imagine anything else.

A way of life, like a huge boulder lying motionless on the ground, takes enormous effort to get rolling. But, once it gains momentum, it is a formidable force.

You have invested your entire life in getting and keeping your rock rolling. It is what we do as humans. Move relentlessly forward, one step at a time. Maybe you have begun to ask the dreaded questions, "Am I going in the right direction? Is this the life that I imagined I would live?" In merely asking the questions, you have opened your possibilities for change. Contented people rarely ask these questions.

Have questions of purpose and direction been knocking at your door? Have you looked in the distance at the approaching horizon and yearned to take a different path, to change directions? Some course corrections are minor and the rolling rock you ride can navigate the small turn easily. Some changes require a complete stop and the strength to begin again. Some even require convincing others. You do not ride that rock alone. Family members and friends are very invested in the life you have created with them and may not want you changing the game.

But, in truth, it is your rock to roll, your life to live. Watching your dreams fade in the distance as you move further and further away makes life dreary and meaningless. Even if others want you to stay the course, for their own selfish reasons, they will eventually be left holding a vacant shell of you. They will lose and you will lose.

You are already a fair bit down the path. Momentum has built. The way is established and the destination is obvious. Are you excited about your direction or living in dread of its inevitable conclusion? A reader found that her life direction was leading her to an end that was meaningless for her and she set out to align her path with her values.

"For most of my life I bought into what everyone else expected of me, or in truth, what I *thought* they expect of me. I realized there was NO satisfaction in that. It was a self-destructive goal that I would never achieve.

I started to take stock of what my success factors truly were. Not what I thought they should be. I found that my success factors centered less on material desires and focused more on spiritual and emotional values. They centered on my faith in God and Jesus. From there I focused on close personal relationships with family and dear friends. I began to realize that life was temporal and fleeting, and that I needed to focus on the things that would endure long after the money and prestige were spent.

I felt a strong need to be in a position of giving back and getting in tune with other people's deepest feelings. I wanted to be able to help others through their hurts and to be a calming influence in their lives. When I stepped back and looked at my life, I was none of those things. I was so unhappy trying to please everyone and working toward unrealistic expectations that I had created for myself. I had lost sight of what really mattered to me.

I'd considered going back to school for a counseling or a psychology degree, but I didn't want to have to start all over in a new career. Part of what I wanted in this transition was more quality time with my husband and family. I had been a Marketing Product Manager for a large company as well as many other corporate jobs. When I was chasing the almighty dollar, I was commuting far, working late, being stressed, and being unfulfilled. I spent an immense amount of time in prayer asking God to help me align my faith and my profession, to have happiness and peace with where I was, and still earn a living, as well as work close to home.

I kept thinking this is an awful tall order to fill. How will this ever come to be? Then when I had exhausted attempts to find happiness in various jobs that did not fulfill these innermost needs, I gave up my expectations and thoughts of what should happen and trusted that something would happen. I didn't try to piece together the entire puzzle. I defined the important touch points to me, and then I lifted it up in prayer and let it go.

To my surprise, I heard of an opening for the Office Administrator at my church. Never had I ever dreamed of being a church secretary. It took some mental adjustment, having been a Marketing Product Manager and Project Manager to say, 'I am a secretary,' much less, a church secretary.

However, it was the answer to all my prayers: earning a living; aligning my work and my faith; working closer to home with a two minute commute if the light was red; more time with my family and close friends; and a sense of inner peace. I cannot tell you how much happier I am in this role, doing something that gives back to the community and to individuals, than when I was trying to fulfill self-imposed, unrealistic expectations. What a freeing experience this has been. I am free to be the person that I wanted to be rather than who I thought I was supposed to be." —Donna Dehne

Donna realized that her energies had been aimed at rolling a rock that wasn't hers. One that didn't fulfill her real desires. So, she stopped pushing and looked for a truer path. She broke the momentum of her life to find a new direction. Would it have been any easier had she pursued this change earlier than she did? It's hard to say. Momentum creates such a compelling force for continuance.

The thing about momentum is that it never does get easier to stop. Waiting another day only wastes another day. It puts you that much further down the wrong path. Today is as easy as it will ever be to change directions. Decide today to save yourself and your dreams. You are the only one who can. Dig in your heels and the boulder *will* stop. Use the strength of your dreams to turn it around and begin again fresh, renewed in faith, and confident that each push moves you closer to your destiny.

Even if you are feeling exhausted now, you do have the strength to change course. Fulfilling the wrong destiny is exhausting and that is what saps your energy. Doing what you love is invigorating. That is where the strength to make a course correction will come from. Never fear, your strength to change is there.

Each morning remember what you want and why you want it. Let your dreams fill you with commitment and passion. If momentum slows and inertia eats at your resolve, envision the conclusion of your chosen path and savor the sweetness of faithfulness to the dream.

"What I have learned and continue to discover is that I'm giving birth to unconditional self-acceptance, a sense of humor I never knew I had, unbelievable strength, courage beyond my imagination, unrelenting perseverance, and surrender borne of a desperate need for peace. In those Zen moments of being detached from my personal experience, I feel myself chuckling at the paradox that embraces this time of life. I am falling apart to come together!"
—Sandy Kay

In the end, it is your choice, it is your life. What will you do with it? That is the only question you are here to answer. How will you choose to live your life? Are you stuck in a rut of obedience to your doubt and fear? Are you deliberately doing what you need to do to make your dreams come alive?

Live courageously and follow your heart. There is less time left than you think. You do not have the luxury to dawdle anymore? Let your dreams take flight. Others may object, at first, because you are changing the game. When they see you blossom, they will know that your win is their win too. Who knows, they might even shed their own comfort and join you.

What if you find that where you are and where you're going isn't the destiny you wish, but you know the timing isn't right to make a change? I'm not advocating procrastination, but sometimes, even if we know we *will* make a change, we recognize that to do so right now would create more problems than staying the course just a bit more. How do you find any sense of happiness or fulfillment pushing what you know is the wrong rock?

In the next chapter, It's What You Give, we'll wake up to a knowing that can make all the difference in your sense of peace, even while biding your time for change. It is a secret that if known by more, would revolutionize the workplace and relationships.

20   It's What You Give

"Don't waste life in doubts and fears; spend yourself on the work before
you, well assured that the right performance of this hour's duties will be
the best preparation for the hours and ages that will follow it."
—Ralph Waldo Emerson

*Author's Note: Is work a snooze? Find out how to turn even a boring job
into a personal joy.*

If I asked you who do you work for, how would you respond?
Notice that I did not ask who pays your salary. Those can be, and
often are, very different questions. The real key to happiness is
recognizing that, although we may apply our skills and time to a company position, every task we do and every goal we achieve is ultimately done for our own growth and fulfillment.

Somewhere between breakfast and the evening news some of us
have lost track of why we do what we do. We just show up, get
through the day, and thank God when the week is over. Hence, the
often heard sigh of relief, "Thank God it's Friday" (TGIF). Usually followed two days later by the dispirited groan of, "Oh, God, it's
Monday."

These are the battle cries of indentured workers who sell their time
for money in the hope that someday they'll have enough money so
they can, ironically, buy back the remainder of their lives. Forty years
of work in exchange for twenty years of retirement . . . if they're lucky.
The deck is definitely stacked in favor of the company.

It can be different. No, you do not have to quit your job . . .
although if you hate it, that might not be a bad place to start. Even if
you keep the job, the secret between a wildly satisfying life and one of
seeming slavery is a simple shift of thought.

Let me ask the question again. Who do you work for? If you
answered with any other name than your own, you have found the
reason why so many are unhappy at work. I am not espousing self-
employment; not in the way you probably think of it. Regardless of
who pays your salary, truly, your happiness lies in the acknowledge-
ment that you ultimately work for you.

The difference is subtle, but powerful. Let's say that you do not like
or even respect your boss. Each day you do your job while harboring
the resentment that you have to put up with the *jerk*. You do what you
must to meet your goals, but aren't about to give him/her your all.
They don't deserve your best, right? You figure the less you invest yourself there the better. Your motto is to just get the paycheck and go home.

If you do not feel this way at the moment, chances are you recognize the situation. What is it like to live like that? Exhausting. Frustrating. Degrading. It poisons your sleep and drains your ambition. Next time you are riding the elevator on a Monday morning, look around closely and you'll see them—the walking dead who bring their bodies to work, but leave their spirits at home. They punch the clock and hold on until the end of the day. These are workers who only see work as a means to an end. They choose to do their living on the weekends and get through the week with as little effort as possible.

So, how can you keep your job, work for the same *jerk*, and go home every night feeling invigorated and fulfilled? Simply remember that regardless of what *they* expect or experience of your work, you are the person who most needs to be impressed with your results. The quality of your work is a direct reflection of the respect you have for yourself. Intentionally doing a shoddy job makes you feel like a shoddy person. Purposefully withholding your best reduces you to a faint shadow of who you really are. Everyone loses, you most of all.

I would be willing to bet that the times you feel highly energized and most fulfilled in your work are the times when you go all-out. You give it everything you've got because you are fully invested in the outcome and you want to hit a homerun. That level of contribution feels so personally rewarding that the day seems to fly by and it's tough to stop and go home. You're actually having *that* much fun!

It feels good to do good work. Your work reflects who you believe you are, not just what you do, but *how* you do it. It doesn't matter what the job is, you always have the choice of doing it well or doing it carelessly. Those who chose to do a job well, regardless of the circumstances, do it because they take great pride in doing their best. They know that giving it their all rewards them far beyond any monetary incentives or accolades their employer might bestow.

You deserve your best. Whether it is cleaning the bathroom or presenting your report. The quality of your work speaks for the pride you have in yourself. The bonus you receive is that you will find enormous energy and excitement in the act of excelling. There is a big difference between people who go home exhausted from investing their all in their work and those who drag home after having done as little as possible. It is like exercise. Physical exercise energizes. The more you give the more you have to give.

Who do you work for? No one but you. Are you proud of your efforts? Are you engaged? Do you like what your work says about who you are? The quality of your contribution is a simple choice that makes a huge difference in your experience of life.

The level of your efforts should have nothing to do with how much you like your job or respect your boss. It has everything to do with how much you respect yourself. Do not wait to do great things until you have great work to do. The universe will not bless you with great work to do if you can't even be trusted to do the work you already have with excellence.

This story is from a reader who took personal pride in his level of dedication and achievement in working for his employer. For years his high commitment was well rewarded, but the company changed, and he found himself faced with a self defining decision that would change the course of his life.

"I spent my whole thirty-year working career with one company. For the most part, it was a great company to work for. In the beginning, I gave it my all and did everything I possibly could to help it succeed. Being very ambitious, I worked excessive hours and traveled between sixty and eighty percent of the time. I was totally dedicated and loyal to this company. I received several promotions that also included relocations and ultimately ending up at the corporate headquarters. However, my personal life suffered because my career was my first priority. In retrospect, I would have chosen more balance in my life from a personal-business perspective.

I always conducted business with a high degree of ethics and integrity. I respected those people that I was associated with. As a leader, I followed the golden rule of management religiously: *take care of your people, treat them well, and they will go to the ends of the earth for you.* I've always received positive feedback from my employees and business partners about my management style and how I conducted business. I consistently received great performance reviews and was always in the excelled category.

The company sold my business unit to an international firm nine years ago and everything changed. In most cases, change is needed and is usually for the positive. However, in this case, changes that were taking place were not good and the overall philosophy toward

"I'm Catholic and I was raised Catholic and taught by Jesuits. The Jesuits are very much intellectual disciplinarians. One of the things that they really instilled in us was the requirement that, as a person in society, one must serve. That that's really where joy comes in life, from serving.

I've gotten back to that. I've spent a long time serving a small number of business clients and growing their businesses for them through my efforts in marketing and communications and that's fine. I was adequately compensated for that effort. But, there's a bigger arena and a bigger opportunity out there to serve a lot of people. I've been given pretty substantial gifts, I think, and I feel that there is a lot expected of me. So I'm off on that adventure trying to live up to an expectation that may be, merely, mine."
—Chris Needler

employees changed drastically for the worse. The new company didn't care about the employees and were only *bottom-line* oriented.

It was heart wrenching to watch the changes over time and see veteran workers being laid off. Many had been loyal, productive and results-oriented employees who had dedicated their lives to the company. I became very angry and frustrated watching how hurt and devastated these employees were. I lost a lot of sleep. I felt so sorry for them and their families that my stress level raised and my blood pressure did too. My feelings for this company were changing by the minute. I was becoming angrier and angrier.

A new team of young, inexperienced managers was put into place. Their decisions were not in the best interest of the company or our customers. I approached the senior management team on several occasions to let them know that we had made those same decisions in prior years and the results had been devastating. They didn't believe me and continued their plans. The end result occurred exactly as I had told them.

The senior management team then started to get more involved in *my* business and my department. I was the largest revenue producer for all the sales regions; however, they made me review all plans with them prior to implementing and every decision I proposed was declined. Their decisions hurt my department, but after fighting them as much as I could, they forced my compliance.

Their way of doing business would compromise my ethics and integrity in dealing with our partners. I refused. I was not going to jeopardize the outstanding reputation internally and externally I had with my customers and partners. I had to look myself in the mirror. I refused to change who I am. At the end of that year I received the worst performance review in my life. It was painful and frustrating. I have always been a strong, results-oriented performer; having received several awards, bonuses and special recognition over the years. My personnel file had numerous letters of recommendations, accomplishments and awards. I made the special sales clubs for top performers several times. This review was just devastating to me. I knew then that this was the beginning of the end.

My personality began to change. I wasn't a fun-loving, outgoing person any more. I withdrew and became quiet and reclusive. I knew I had to make a change, any change, to get out of this environment. Then one day, management told me that I was no longer employed. I couldn't believe it. I don't know how I kept my composure, but I did. I felt empty and worthless. I was hurt, upset, frustrated, and angry and couldn't understand how this had happened to me.

My self-confidence was shaken, but I received tremendous support from my wife, family and friends who helped me pull through this devastating event. My colleagues, customers, and partners told me that they had only done business with this company because of my honesty and integrity.

In retrospect, I know that I made the right decision not to compromise my values, ethics, and integrity. Yes, it cost me my job and my lifetime career, but I kept my self-worth. I know, with confidence, that I conducted my business affairs with fairness, integrity, and honesty, and that the decisions that I made were in the best interest of the company, our customers and partners.

I can look myself in the mirror with self-respect and know that I made the right choices in my life. Now I will move forward to another chapter in my life."—Reader

This man was employed by others, but he never lost track of the truth that his work was, foremost, a declaration of who he was—a statement to the world of his values and self-respect. When faced with the choice to satisfy the external world or retain his integrity, he knew that being true to his self worth was more than any external rewards.

Today, even in small ways, leave your stamp on what you touch. Even if no one else sees it, make it your best work anyway. It is the level of your contribution that determines the level of your satisfaction in life. As Winston Churchill proclaimed, "We make a living by what we get, but we make a life by what we give."

Living in the world at this level of integrity is self honoring. Yet, it also honors others by contributing our service with love, because, in the end, we are all one people and one spirit. It's good to remember that the real reward in life comes when we give everything we've got to everything we do, to our work and to our relationships. In the next chapter, The Faces of Love, we'll see that all of life comes down to relationships: the one we have with our self and the ones we share with others.

21 The Faces of Love

"Where there is love there is life."
–Mohandas K. Gandhi

Author's Note: Family squabbles? See how love makes all else meaningless.

Six bags of liquid dripped into six plastic tubes draining into the needle in her neck. The breathing tube invading her throat often caused her to gag and gasp for air. You could see the panic on her face when she thought she was suffocating.

This is how I found my aunt in the early hours of a solemn winter morning. Three hours earlier, Mom had called. She said her sister had relapsed and had been re-admitted to the hospital. Aunt Myrna might be dying. Although it was late at night, Mom was making the drive to Yakima immediately. Living an hour further away, I said I would be right behind her.

Only three weeks earlier, I had heard that Aunt Myrna was feeling ill and her skin was yellowing. The lab tests confirmed autoimmune hepatitis. Her body was rejecting her liver and was shutting down. The natural wastes from digestion and bodily processes could not be removed from her system, and she was slowly being poisoned. She had begun to swell from water retention, but medicines seemed to be working to alleviate her pain.

Just recently she had seemed to be getting much better and was home and getting back to her old life. Two days after being released from the hospital, Myrna relapsed and was rushed to the emergency room unconscious. When Mom called, Myrna was in a coma.

My four-hour drive, in the black of night, felt ominously disengaged from reality. The moonless sky shrouded the land around me in indiscernible shadows and my mind raced with questions I could not answer. Mile upon mile, I was alone on the highway: no headlights coming toward me, no city lights in the distance, and no signs of life. The symbolism didn't go unnoticed.

Occasionally, an 18-wheeler barreled by, jolting my anxious thoughts back from imagining what might happen that day. Most of all, my mind was flooded with worry for my mom. She and Myrna were very close. More than just sisters, they shared a love of quilting that fed their insatiable creativity as well as their special friendship. I knew Mom was panicked, and I could only imagine the dreadful thoughts accompanying her on her solitary drive.

When I arrived at the Critical Care Unit, Mom was alone with her unconscious sister. It was 2:30 a.m. I did not recognize my aunt. A ventilator violently pumped her chest up and down like a lifeless doll. Her arms were a mass of purple and yellow bruises from countless needles. The nurses had resorted to using her neck for the IV's. The overused veins in her arms were too sunken for a needle to penetrate. Her hands were cold and limp. Her vacant eyes a milky yellow.

At seven o'clock family and friends began to arrive. Soon there were over twenty of us. The nurses only allowed two at a time in Myrna's room, so we filled the corridor . . . sitting on the few available chairs and crouching together along the walls of the narrow hallway. Myrna was the only one in the CCU and the nurses did their best to accommodate our growing numbers.

With each passing hour we rode a roller coaster of good news that turned bad, then good again. Two by two we kept vigil: holding her hand, or stroking her hair, speaking our love. Two by two we left sobbing.

The only time Myrna moved was when, in her unconsciousness, she felt the tube down her throat. She would gag, panic, and try to pull the invasive tube from her mouth. But, her arms were strapped to the bed. We tried to reassure her and encourage her to not fight the machine breathing for her. Then the morphine in her system would take hold and she would drift away . . . lifeless again.

At one point I looked at my extended family crowding the halls of the CCU. They were holding each other, talking quietly, and sharing their despair and their love. I have a big family. Mom had twelve siblings and the aunts, uncles, cousins and second cousins were everywhere. Some relatives I didn't recognize; some I had not seen in ten years; some even twenty. Old reminiscences revealed how we each remembered the other. Funny things, odd memories.

What struck me the most was that even though we were practically *strangers*, we found a common bond in our love for the woman in room 443. Those who had barely spoken to each other before this day exchanged sadness and hope, differences faded, petty bickering and judgments ceased. None of that was important here. What was important was sharing our love and support. Nothing else mattered.

My aunt stabilized enough for the doctors to transport her to Seattle. They said that the hospital there was better equipped to treat Myrna's illness. The medics kept us away while they detached all of her tubing and prepped her for the gurney waiting in the hall. When they wheeled her out, however, the nurse asked if we would like to say goodbye. That simple caring gesture spoke volumes about the fragile human connection we all find in grief.

Forming a line, we approached Myrna's tightly wrapped body, kissed her forehead or cheek and said we loved her. The words goodbye just seemed too forbidding to utter. Then she was gone. Off to what we all prayed was only a brief pause in her continued life with us.

A few days later, I heard Myrna was more responsive. The doctors had been unable to stop the bleeding ulcer in her stomach, though. She had received eight units of blood since being readmitted to the hospital. I was not convinced that being more aware was necessarily a good thing for her. Perhaps not knowing what was going on would allow her body to do the healing it needed to do without the worry her mind might cause.

My aunt did not survive more than a few days. Her body simply surrendered. She died with her husband and her children at her side in those final moments of her life. She had lived long enough for so many of her family to be with her one last time and to speak our last words of love. Each of us was reminded that life is fragile and fleeting. We only have each other for a brief time. We cannot allow ourselves to waste that time with anything but love and gratitude and respect.

There were times that early morning while stroking her hair that I saw Myrna open one eye slightly. Even though the opening was tiny, I could feel the enormous connection between us. It was like an electrical surge. I *knew* she saw me, and I smiled through my tears.

Now and then a lone tear would roll down her cheek. I could only imagine her thoughts. I wanted to hold her and tell her it would be all right. This poked and prodded, swollen-bodied woman was my blood, my mother's sister. Though her body lay lifeless, through the glimmer of a partially opened eye, I could see her invincible spirit.

Promise me this . . . when you finish this story call someone you love and tell them how much they mean to you. You will make two hearts sing.

No matter whom you are angry at, upset at, or holding a grudge against . . . none of that matters if there is one ounce of love between you. Love is *not* conditional. It cannot just be shut off like a faucet. That heart-wrenching night in the CCU, I witnessed love's power in my family. Selfish attitudes and petty criticisms dissolved in tears and hugs that healed old wounds. Love healed it all.

Think seriously about how damaging your quarrel with a loved one can be. Consider how much precious love you are wasting by letting a difference come between you. Believe me, nothing they have done, or you think they have done, will matter one second if they died right now.

Love is the most precious gift we give or receive. Give and receive as much as your heart can hold. Do not wait a moment. That moment may be too long.

Love isn't just an outwardly directed offering. It is also the most priceless gift you can give yourself. Not to be confused with ego, self-love is nurturing and healthy. It is honoring your being and your contributions to the world. It is recognizing that you are a unique presence on the planet and without your contribution, we would all be less.

In the following chapter, we'll examine the vital nature of following your passion, not just to your own fulfillment, but also to the evolution of humankind. To have a gift and not give it is the most sorrowful act of all . . . for all.

22 I Hope You Dance

"The day came when the risk it took to remain tight in the bud was more painful than the risk it took to blossom."
–Anais Nin

Author's Note: Don't sell out on your dreams. Find real happiness in life by making decisions that say, "This is who I am!"

So, you say you have a dream, and that you would give anything to live that dream every day? Really? What price are you willing to pay to make that happen? Why haven't you paid it yet?

A few years back I finally decided to let my fermenting dream of being a public speaker and independent business consultant finally see the light of day. I left a job that I enjoyed and pulled up ten year's worth of roots. It was time to move on. It had been time for several years. I returned to my home state that I had left eighteen years before. I moved to a town I had never lived in, where I knew no one, and started a business that would achieve a level of success beyond my hopes in less than a year.

That is the short story. The one that doesn't even hint at the fear, the decisions, or the determination that it took to walk that road. It was not easy. The important things in life rarely are, nor should they be. We always say we want it to be easy, but we never value it when it is. We seem to value most that which we work hard for.

What exactly does it take to live the life of your dreams? Perfect timing? Fortunate opportunities? A million dollars in the bank? Not even close. It takes a decision: a simple decision that will ultimately test the strength of your commitment and the depth of your faith.

After leaving California, I temporarily moved back in with Mom. It was a soft place to land while I tried to figure out, now that I had stepped into my future, exactly what that future would look like. You see, my dream had inspired me enough to get out of the situation I had been in, but now that I had taken the first leap, I wasn't exactly sure what I was leaping toward. I had planned well for my departure, but no further. Without a real plan for moving forward, I began to have second thoughts. I felt lost somewhere between my past and the future.

In this place of *in between*, I lost my momentum and my resolve. The road before me looked much longer and rockier than I had imagined. I was not sure I had what it would take to be successfully independent. I began to look back on the comfortable life I had left and wondered if I had made the right decision. What if I couldn't get clients? Maybe

I would not be able to make enough money to pay my bills. What if my new town did not want me? What if I lost everything? What if I had to live with my mother for the rest of my life?

Well, one thought led to another and pretty soon fear was my constant companion. I was virtually paralyzed and could not get any mental traction to move forward. Then, like the trickster life is, within days I received a phone call from a very large, very successful company saying they wanted to interview me for a management training and development position. Management training had been my previous career. I had forgotten all about the resume I had mailed to them eight months earlier.

My heart beat a little faster as I saw a way out of the spiraling panic of an undefined future. This position was a way back to something familiar to stand on. I flew to Seattle and wowed them during the six hours of interviews! Smiles were abundant and references to next steps flowed freely. On the trip home there was no doubt in my mind that they would offer me the job. It was a great company with good people in a terrific city. I was ecstatic.

Sure enough, two days later the call came. I had the job. I fought my urge to accept immediately and told them I would call them back the next day with an answer. Why did I hesitate? I wasn't quite sure at that very moment.

The thrill of being *wanted* kept me high all afternoon. I talked at length with my mom about what I would be doing for the company. I told her about my new boss and what she was like. I considered where I might like to live. I wondered if I could take a week or two to move before starting my new responsibilities. I was off and running with the new development and all the inertia I had felt for the past few months had vanished in the flurry of my excitement.

That is when the almost forgotten dream scratched at the back door of my mind. "What about me?" it whispered. It was faint, but powerful. Part of me did not want to hear it. Unlike the Seattle job, the dream was unknown. Unlike the Seattle job, the dream was unclear. The dream was frightening, but it was *insistent*.

Why had I uprooted my life in California to pursue a dream of independence only to succumb to a mirror image of my previous life in California? Though momentarily forgotten, the dream was unrelenting. I had two options; two destinies. I had to choose one.

Standing at the fork of that decision was one of the hardest things I have ever done. One road led me to security and familiarity. The paycheck would come in each week. I would be doing what I knew and was good at. Life could get back to some degree of regularity. Comfort was just around the corner.

The other fork led to the imagined dream. I could not see down the road very far. Uncertainty and potential risk lived in that neighborhood. There may be all manner of beasts waiting to gobble me up for breakfast. I had no guarantee of success. Fear slithered back into my heart and I froze . . . unable to see beyond the worry.

In that mire of confusion, a small voice arose and it shook its bony little finger at me and scolded, "If you don't even *try* to make your dream happen, you will always know you sold yourself out!"

There it was—the moment of truth. What was my life all about? Was it about being safe or tasting life's bounty? Was it about crawling in the rut or bounding over hilltops? I could have whatever I chose, but I had to choose. And I had to do it now.

I took a hard look in the mirror and realized I could only make one choice. I chose not to let fear make my decisions. I chose not to retreat, but to advance . . . into whatever life might have waiting. It is a choice I remake every day. It gets a little easier each time, a little.

We are all going to die someday and there is nothing we can do about that. Playing it safe or not in life, it will not make a speck of difference. You cannot avoid risk by standing still. As a matter of fact, standing still makes you a sitting target. We all know what happens to sitting targets!

With every decision you make, you either choose to live or to die; to move toward something or to run away from something; or to let your divine passion steer your course or to bow to fear.

"Karen's insight into life and its wonders and the monumental capabilities, that we as human beings possess, has affected me deeply. Her tender, persistent prodding encouraged me to not just live, but to excel, enjoy, and consider my potential rather than my shortcomings. Her writing is like a literary river that slowly, but persistently, wore away my doubts, blame and anger." —Al O.

Let your dreams and passions pull you toward your heart's desire. That is the purpose of dreams and passions! Make decisions that enhance your self-esteem and your quality of life. Reach high and I promise you, there is more waiting for you than you can even imagine. Your wildest hopes are trivial compared to what is possible for you.

Resolve to not sell out on yourself. You are the vehicle of your dream's incarnation. No one else can make it happen. Decide to live large and taste everything you can. That is why we are here. That is what life is.

In the process of following your dream you will grow. It's one of life's little ironies. We think we are after a dream and we keep our focus outward. In truth, we are seeking to return to our spiritual wholeness, we can evolve into the next level of life. The dream we have for our lives isn't the goal, it's the means to our spiritual growth. We achieve that growth whether the dream is realized or not. Even when the dream fails, sometimes especially when the dream fails, we grow deeper in our understanding of ourselves. We win no matter what. As long as we engage in life, no moment is worthless.

Each day we are asked to join in the dance of life. Sometimes it's exhilarating and fun; other times it's painful and confusing. But, regardless of how it feels, the only way we grow is to participate. We're here to live, not to hold back. To watch from the sidelines only guarantees regret. So, what will *you* do? At the end of our lives, only we will know the choices we have made—the times we jumped in and the times we hesitated too long—the people we let in and the love we let pass—the gratitude we felt and the peace we found. When it's all said and done, I hope you choose to dance!

23   It Is Enough

"The great teachings unanimously emphasize that all the peace, wisdom, and joy in the universe are already within us; we don't have to gain, develop, or attain them. We're like a child standing in a beautiful park with his eyes shut tight. We don't need to imagine trees, flowers, deer, birds, and sky; we merely need to open our eyes and realize what is already here, who we really are —as soon as we quit pretending we're small or unholy."
—Unknown

Author's Note: In our desire to have more, we can too easily forget all that we already have. It's good to remember that gratitude not only gives, it also attracts more.

Today is a day for celebration, for no reason really. I haven't won the lottery or made a new friend. It's just that the sun is shining brightly on my potted daisies; the breeze is running its fingers through the swaying pine trees; and I am upright and breathing. Sometimes it doesn't take much to sink into the arms of blissful gratitude.

We too easily overlook some of the most wondrous things that make living such a miraculous phenomenon. Every day we are presented with endless reasons to be joyful, if we simply notice.

I invite you to join me and take a moment to thank life for the marvels in your day.

You have all the air you can breathe and nourishing food to keep your body healthy.

You have people who believe you are their dream come true.

You have a quick mind that gets you through the obstacle course of your day, every day.

You have keen senses to witness the wondrous miracle of nature.

You have warmth to give to another and arms to receive it in return.

You have an imagination that weaves wispy threads of fantasy to endlessly entertain you.

"The true appreciation of my blessings comes in the quiet moments: taking an evening walk with my husband; sharing a cup of tea with a friend; or chuckling at the silly grin of contentment on the cat's face as she lies purring in my lap. Things click into place and I am filled with a glow of gratitude that whatever else is going on in my life that I will have to deal with again later, in this moment, for this little while, all is well and I am all right. I haven't yet mastered the ability to call that feeling up at will when I need it most, but I'm working on it, and perhaps with God's help I'll manage it eventually."
—Tracy H.

You have language to whisper sweet nothings in a loved one's ear.

You have laughter to lift the spirits of the lonely and tickle the funny bone of a child.

You have a burning passion to make a difference in the lives of others; some you may have never met.

You have wealth surpassing most of the world's comprehension.

You have the Creator's masterpiece spread generously before your eyes at sunset.

You have quiet in which to find yourself.

You have choices to make and things to decide. Not all have these blessings.

You have today.

When your hectic pace and problem riddled life feels like too much to bear, remember the special gifts that always surround you. Stop and notice. Life is full. You won't know that unless you open your eyes and slow your pace.

Your life is precious.

It is beautiful

It is a miracle.

It is enough.